Queer Approaches in
Musical Theatre

Forthcoming in the series:

Hip-Hop in Musical Theater by Nicole Hodges Persley
Race in American Musical Theater by Josephine Lee

Queer Approaches in Musical Theatre

Ryan Donovan

methuen | drama

LONDON • NEW YORK • OXFORD • NEW DELHI • SYDNEY

METHUEN DRAMA
Bloomsbury Publishing Plc
50 Bedford Square, London, WC1B 3DP, UK
1385 Broadway, New York, NY 10018, USA
29 Earlsfort Terrace, Dublin 2, Ireland

BLOOMSBURY, METHUEN DRAMA and the Methuen Drama logo are
trademarks of Bloomsbury Publishing Plc

First published in Great Britain 2023

Series design by Rebecca Heselton

A catalogue record for this book is available from the British Library.

A catalog record for this book is available from the Library of Congress.

ISBN: PB: 978-1-3502-4762-8
ePDF: 978-1-3502-4763-5
eBook: 978-1-3502-4764-2

Series: Topics in Musical Theatre

Typeset by Deanta Global Publishing Services, Chennai, India
Printed and bound in Great Britain

To find out more about our authors and books visit www.bloomsbury.com
and sign up for our newsletters.

Contents

Introduction

Queerness's ever-shifting status onstage and off can be gleaned, in part, by how musicals include it. For an example, let's look at two notable moments from vastly different eras where public displays of affection reveal much about how musicals approach queer love. *The Prom* (2018) ends triumphantly with two teenage girlfriends sharing a kiss at their prom and singing and dancing happily ever after. This happy ending contrasts with that of the *La Cage aux Folles* (1981), which concludes with the middle-aged long-term gay couple at the show's center reprising their romantic duet "Song on the Sand." The stage directions indicate, "(They are dancing now, and we are back in the original square. Lights glow in the building windows. As the buildings close around ALBIN and GEORGES, little slivers of moonlight float down on them and . . .) THE CURTAIN FALLS."[1] They did not kiss and likely could not have then.[2] On Broadway a kiss is *not* just a kiss—especially when it involves queer coupling. The divergent representations of these couples mark shifts in the relationship of queerness and musicals that this book will chart; while musicals embrace queerness more than ever, this relationship was historically ambivalent at times, haltingly inclusive at others, and openly exclusionary at others.

Queerness in musicals doesn't only exist in couples, though. But because of the slant toward heteronormative romance that most musicals have historically shown, queer approaches have often reiterated the imperative to couple off and live happily ever after. Sometimes, however, musicals have killed off their queer characters before the curtain falls, foreclosing the possibility of happily ever after. Musicals act as barometers of their specific cultural contexts—in other words, how musicals represent queerness, who performs in them, who writes them, who stages them, who markets them, and who sees them all have something to tell you about musicals and the world beyond them.

The fact that one short book can no longer address or contain all of the queer approaches in and to musical theatre is commendable for a form that historically closeted queer sexualities and genders. The fact that there are now more shows than can fit here is a profound measure of change. This book primarily addresses Broadway and West End musicals, and though queer approaches to musicals exist beyond those commercial enclaves, I am most concerned here with how queerness exists and persists in mainstream US and UK commercial theatre. Regional theatres have also pushed the proverbial envelope of representation to produce queer interpretations of classic musicals, like Oregon Shakespeare Festival's genderqueer *Oklahoma!* in 2018.[3] In the UK, queer musicals like *Everybody's Talking About Jamie* (2017) regularly premiere in regional theatres outside of the West End before sometimes transferring there. The explosion of queer approaches to musical theatre, especially in and after the 1990s, reflected, and in some cases anticipated and on others followed, the newly increasing representation in culture and media, greater social acceptance and growing political power of queer people.

Musical theatre was historically a space where queer people could be taken seriously offstage, even if the form itself often caricatured or lampooned queerness onstage. For decades, the association of queerness and musicals pointed largely in one direction in practice and in theory: toward white gay men. If musicals themselves would go on to cement this connection onstage, it is not exactly an accurate representation of the long history of queers and musicals. Queerness hasn't always been male or white in musicals, though: consider the fact that Ethel Waters, a bisexual Black actor and singer, was one of the highest paid Broadway stars in the 1940s.[4] Waters was necessarily closeted then—as nearly all queer people were—and married to a man, but her relationship with dancer Ethel Williams in the 1920s was something of an open secret. It still took decades for musicals to include queer characters beyond white male roles, which were often in drag, before newer ways of categorizing gender (e.g., cis, trans, non-binary) became common. Roles for queer performers who aren't white are still relatively scarce; for every Celie in *The Color Purple* (2005) or Usher in *A Strange Loop* (2022)—two of a handful of leading roles both Black and queer—there are dozens of roles for white gay men. This gap reflects the intersection of homophobia, transphobia, misogyny, and racism that exists within professional theatre and society at large. Queerness in musical theatre have not always been so inclusive.

Musical theatre began to forge new frontiers in more inclusive, if often imperfect, gender representation largely after 2010; On Broadway this was seen in *Bring It On* (2012) and Off-Broadway in *Southern Comfort* (2016), which both featured trans characters, as well as the West End hit *& Juliet* (2019), which features queer and nonbinary characters who get happy endings. But for every show like *Jagged Little Pill* (2019) and *Some Like It Hot* (2022), where characters grapple with understanding their own gender, there seems to be yet another musical using the "man in a dress" trope like *Tootsie* (2019) and *Mrs. Doubtfire* (2021). Queer representation in musicals is simultaneously contracting and expanding—and the co-existence of all of the musicals mentioned in this paragraph shows that musical theatre is a site where gender's performance gets worked out onstage, much like musicals worked out queer sexuality in earlier decades.

Some of the roots of the expansion of queer representation can be found in the 1970s: the first lesbian love song in a Broadway musical was in Melvin Van Peeble's musical *Ain't Supposed to Die a Natural Death* (1971), which featured a Black woman singing out to her incarcerated lover in the women's prison at "Tenth and Greenwich." This song preceded the first gay male romantic song on Broadway, "Why Can't the World Go and Leave Us Alone?" from *Dance a Little Closer* (1983). *New York Times* critic Frank Rich noted that this was sung by "a caricatured homosexual couple who do a gratuitous ice-skating number."[5] Both of these songs relied on stereotypes to a degree (associating lesbians with a women's prison and gay men with ice skating), and yet both marked definite advances in queer representation for their time.

Queer Approaches in Musical Theatre introduces readers to a facet of musicals often assumed yet misrecognized: that queerness and musical theatre's relationship extends much deeper than camp fabulosity and reveals, at times, a stark ambivalence. Queer approaches in musical theatre often challenge heteronormativity but sometimes subtly reinforce it. Queerness in musical theatre exists beyond familiar narratives of gay men's over-representation onstage and offstage. The status of queerness and musical theatre's relationship is perhaps best summed up by admitting, "It's complicated." Yet we must ask what makes a queer approach—the queerness of the musical's subject or its creators or its actors or its audience or all of the above? And who gets to decide the answers to these questions? This book will address many of the facets of this special relationship as well as the contradictions and tension that exist between musicals and queer approaches to critiquing, creating, producing, writing, and viewing them.

This book offers ways of studying musicals centered on four case studies and demonstrates that queerness can be a powerful lens to use in order to understand the world through understanding musicals and vice versa. The case studies that follow focus on historical context, text, staging and production, and reception. The historical context study addresses the impact of AIDS on musical theatre and the onstage treatment of AIDS in musicals. A close examination of the text of Lisa Kron and Jeanine Tesori's musical *Fun Home* (2015) follows. I then turn to the staging and production of *Cabaret* (1966) and its ever-evolving ways of incorporating queerness in revivals. The final case study examines differences in the reception of *La Cage aux Folles* (1983) between the gay press and the mainstream press.

But before we delve into the case studies and the selected musicals, we first must appreciate the territory—and the ever-shifting terminology—we are going to survey. To do so, we'll first look at the word *queer* itself, then take a quick look at queerness in early twentieth-century US and UK theatre, proceed on to how the press framed queer issues in print, then see how scholars have studied musicals and queerness. Queer approaches in and to musical theatre must grapple with the fact that representation differs quite profoundly from inclusion. Musicals are a place like no other where queerness exerts itself.

What Is Queer?

Perhaps the most salient defining feature of the word *queer* is the very difficulty of defining it. Queer is a slippery term, ever-accruing new meanings. It has alternately indicated strangeness and/or otherness, been a term of identification and/or a slur, in addition to a verb, a noun, and an adjective. According to the Oxford English Dictionary, *queer* has, well, a queer history. It has been in usage in various forms since *c.* 1390, when it initially meant to question, later morphing to mean "bad, counterfeit, forged," or "living dishonestly" before settling on "strange, odd, peculiar" in the sixteenth century and then as a derogatory term for homosexual in the early twentieth.[6] In the 1980s and 1990s, the reclamation of the term by gay activists and advocates was underway, paving the way for newer usages. The indefinite article's relationship to queer also determines its meaning and its context: usage shifted from *a* queer to simply *queer* as signifier of collective political identity rather than a stigmatized individual identity.

Perhaps the simplest way to begin to define queer is by naming what it is not (or at least previously was not): heteronormative. Heteronormativity, as queer theorist David M. Halperin outlines it, "is a system of norms connected with a particular form of life, a form of life that comprises a number of interrelated elements, all of them fused into a single style of social existence."[7] This social existence culminates in marriage and procreation, cementing the nuclear family and its associated norms of gender and sexuality. But heteronormativity extends beyond just enforcing norms of gender and sexuality, it imposes "models of appropriate community membership, of public speech and self-representation, political participation, freedom, family life, class identity, education, consumption and desire, social display, public culture, racial and national fantasy, health and bodily bearing, trust and truth."[8] Queerness, in this light, presents a challenge to heteronormativity's dominance. If heteronormativity must be reckoned with, then so must homonormativity.

Queer theorist Lisa Duggan's concept of homonormativity (coined in 2002) critiqued some gays and lesbians' embrace of heteronormative norms, which she argued was a result of neoliberal capitalism.[9] Queers made good consumers, which in turn made them good citizens and good candidates for marriage and parenthood. Homonormativity thus recreated for queer people many of the norms of heteronormativity and offered them inclusion into the oppressive structures and systems, either as a way of remaking these systems from within (to note one point of view) or capitulating to them (to note another). That homonormativity could even exist at all was a measure of the increasing social status of gays and lesbians in the early twenty-first century. Homonormativity's emphasis on the politics of "equality" and what was then widely called "gay marriage" meant that it privileged "upper-middle-class, white and otherwise 'normative' LGBTIQ persons who already have a great deal of cultural capital and mobility."[10] Homonormativity points to the fact that though queerness may be something various communities share, it does not necessarily create bonds or communities across other kinds of differences. We must also consider how musicals themselves might reflect and/or enforce homonormativity.

The association of queer with nonconforming sexuality is both historic and ongoing, and, for some, an incomplete or inadequate lens through which to understand the term and who it represents. Yet the radical inclusivity of the term itself has given way to an unexpected (yet also somehow predictable) turn, as *New York Times* writer Jenna Wortham noted in 2016. Wortham writes, "'queer' has come to serve as a linguistic catchall for this broadening spectrum of identities, so much so that people who consider themselves straight, but reject heteronormativity, might even call themselves queer. But when everyone can be queer, is anyone?"[11] The mainstream's desire to usurp, absorb, and commodify difference reveals itself in the rebranding of queer as alternately a marker of urban style—giving rise to neologisms like *metrosexual* and television programs like *Queer Eye for the Straight Guy* (2003–7)—and a rejection of seemingly rigid identity categories like straight and gay and the gender binary (due in large part to queer theorist Judith Butler's paradigm-shifting works like 1990's *Gender Trouble*).

But then what might all of this mean for musicals, a historically gay form but not necessarily always a queer one. For the purposes of this book, I will use the term *queer* within a somewhat narrower definition tied to LGBTQ+ identity since that is generally how musicals have approached queerness. Yet since musicals themselves are exceedingly heteronormative, how do queer approaches in and to them even function? Musicals are the most financially lucrative of theatrical forms for producers, they are popular the world over, and are thus unabashedly capitalist—all of which rather flies in the face of queerness. Or does it? Musicals force us to ask whether queerness and capitalism can comfortably co-exist as well as to consider what role mainstream culture plays and the historical implications of this tension.

Early Examples of Queerness and Musical Theatre

Journalists, historians, and biographers alike have undertaken the work of reconstructing theatre's queer pasts. This section will chart some of the ways that queerness and musical theatre co-existed in the decades before gay liberation in the 1970s burst open the closet doors in new ways. The passing of the Wales Padlock Law in New York City in 1927 meant that plays and musicals could not include openly homosexual characters due to the moral outrage over drag and homosexuality that Mae West's 1927 play *The Drag* had caused among those inclined toward moral outrage at such things. In order to forcefully deter so-called immorality onstage, "the law calls for the arrest . . . of every one in any way connected with the production."[12] That the law was not repealed until 1967 did not mean homosexuals stopped being represented or stopped working in New York theatre, but rather that queer representation became coded and queer people remained closeted, publicly at least. In the UK, government censorship of theatre that had been in place since 1737 was only abolished with the Theatres Act 1968. The 1737 law required every play to undergo review and often censorship by the Lord Chamberlain's office. In terms of what this meant to queer representation, it was similar to what happened in the United States, where coding and camp became common.

Camp's history in the United Kingdom can be traced earlier than in the United States, as theatre scholar Robert Gordon explains, "From at least the early nineteenth century, however, a strain of drollery can be identified in popular English culture that we might today recognize as camp." Gordon goes on to note, "This tradition of facetious mockery only becomes visible as part of a homosexual subculture in the 1890s when the flamboyant dandyism of the Wildean decadent begins to be imitated through its louchely parodic performance ('se camper') by working-class homosexuals."[13] Irish playwright Oscar Wilde's 1895 arrest for "gross indecency" set the stage for queer British theatre artists to remain closeted for decades even as it paradoxically uncloseted male homosexuality. As in the United States, queer people could not come out in the United Kingdom because it was not safe to do so and "homosexual men were subject to regular victimization in the early 1950s by the police force."[14] For example, British playwright and musical theatre composer-lyricist Noel Coward (1899–1973) lived his life with a male partner but remained publicly closeted, and only after his death was his sexuality openly acknowledged in print. When celebrated British actor Sir John Gielgud was arrested cruising for sex in 1953, it sent notice to other gay men in theatre to be careful.

Onstage, though, camp was part survival strategy, part aesthetic, and a smart way of evading censorship. Double entendres were clever ways of making jokes that appeared respectable at first glance but carried double meanings. For instance, the West End musical *Salad Days* (1954), by Julian Slade and Dorothy Reynolds, contained instances of the kinds of jokes that the government censor permitted; these kinds of jokes often existed in performance yet not necessarily openly in the text.[15] Even the word *gay* itself was a coded reference, and was "used with apparent innocence" in the musical and had "a double meaning for those in the know" in 1954.[16] As musical theatre historian Bruce Kirle explains, "The closeting of homosexuals that began during the early 1930s led to coding and the use of the double entendre. The antigay laws and regulations turned the double entendre into a strategy to help gay men pass in straight culture."[17] Camp and double entendres allowed for queerness to hide in plain sight but still retain plausible deniability and offer gay men a measure of defense against censors.

Before the Wales Padlock Law passed in New York, though, "drag and 'pansy' performers were popular in nightclubs in Greenwich Village" in the 1920s, while uptown, plays like Edouard Bourdet's *The Captive* (1926) featured an "offstage homosexual," a convention that "would come to dominate American postwar drama."[18] Tennessee Williams' 1947 play *A Streetcar Named Desire* offers a prime example of the offstage homosexual. Musicals played by somewhat looser rules than drama, though, and slipped queer-coded characters onstage in full view of the morality police without attracting the same amount of attention as straight plays. Musicals like *By Jupiter* (1942) and *Lady in the Dark* (1941) tested the limits of coding and queer representation, the latter in what Kirle calls the "screaming queen" character in fashion photographer Russell Paxton.[19] While Paxton is not an openly gay character, he is clearly coded as such; the stage directions describe him as "the Cecil Beaton of *Allure*. He is still in his early twenties, but very Old World in manner and mildly effeminate in a rather charming fashion." When he first speaks, the directions indicate his affect: "Hysterical, as usual."[20] This description shows precisely how musicals coded queerness in their texts. In performance, it was another matter—Danny Kaye minced and preened his way through the role (as seen in the 1981 television special *Musical Comedy Tonight*, which was hosted by Kaye's wife and featured short excerpts of musicals).[21] Camping on the stage but not the page was a successful strategy, yet also one that reduced gay men to narrow stereotypes. After the 1950s, musicals began to hint more openly, though still not entirely opaquely, at the existence of gay people and subcultures.

Queerness and the Press

If musicals found ways to obliquely include gayness at mid-century, it is instructive to look at how it was—and wasn't—addressed in the mainstream media, which, by extension serve as benchmarks of wider social attitudes and mores, toward both theatre and gays and others perceived as sexual deviants. The *New York Times* has an especially checkered past when it comes to writing about gay issues; its coverage (and lack thereof) reflected and also determined the stigma directed at gays and lesbians during the twentieth century in that the paper helped shape how (and whether) homosexuality was discussed. This was in addition to the role the *Times* played in shaping public perceptions of theatre. In the 1960s, two theatre critics at the *Times* attempted to openly, if indirectly at times, address homosexuality in the theatre—to move beyond coding, as it were. Critic Howard Taubman's 1961 essay, "Not What It Seems: Homosexual Motif Gets Heterosexual Guise" opens with what at first reads like a plea for tolerance: "It is time to speak openly and candidly of the increasing incidence and influence of homosexuality on New York's stage—and, indeed, in the other arts as well." Homosexuality is described as "a difficult, delicate problem" that playwrights problematically represented "in the guise of normality." Taubman notes that although "[h]omosexuality is not a forbidden topic," it must be acknowledged "that heterosexual audiences feel uncomfortable in the presence of truth-telling about sexual deviation" because "even such a theatre must face up to the rules of commerce." Taubman's essay evinces a certain ambivalence about homosexuality:

on the one hand, he does not argue outright that it should be banished from the stage; on the other, he concludes that coded representations "have contaminated some of our arts."[22]

Almost two years later, Taubman felt compelled to write a primer for heterosexual audiences containing "helpful hints on how to scan the intimations and symbols of homosexuality in our theater." He lists a few "obvious" examples, such as the character Charles Marsden in Eugene O'Neill's *Strange Interlude* (1928), and identifies several strategies for the heterosexual spectator to recognize the homosexual; a typical one reads, "Beware the husband who hasn't touched his wife for years." He concludes, "If only we could recover our lost innocence and could believe that people on the stage are what they are supposed to be! Would such a miracle oblige playwrights obsessed by homosexuality and its problems to define their themes clearly and honestly?"[23] Rather than address the conditions that necessitated coding in the first place, coding itself became the issue for Taubman.

Taubman's *Times* colleague Stanley Kauffmann also couched his conflicted views on homosexuality in pleas for more honest representation. His 1966 essay "Homosexual Drama and Its Disguises" became a landmark in theatre criticism for the way he critiqued "the homosexual dramatist" for a lack of openness in an essay in which he himself resorted to innuendo and shied away from naming outright whom he argued was causing theatre's affliction, namely, three gay playwrights: Edward Albee, William Inge, and Tennessee Williams. Kauffmann refers to "normal" playwrights throughout his essay, always in scare quotes. Kauffman, unlike Taubman, notably and laudably blames society for the problem: "If he is to write of his own experience, he must invent a two-sex version of the one-sex experience that he really knows. It is we who insist on it, not he." He concludes, "The conditions that force the dissembling must change. The homosexual dramatist must be free to write truthfully of what he knows, rather than try to transform it to a life he does not know, to the detriment of his truth and ours." Yet in his insistence that gay writers write what only they know, he reduces homosexual artists to being only creators of camp as he essentializes their creations as those that "exalt style, manner, surface."[24] Kauffman's message that society itself is the problem would echo the message of later gay liberationists, and if he was unable to view representations written by gays as anything but vindictive responses to an oppressive society, at least someone at the *Times* was acknowledging the oppression.

Kauffmann's essay drew so many responses from readers that he wrote a response addressing their concerns and laying out his positions more clearly: "The homosexual dramatist ought to have the same freedom that the heterosexual has. While we deny him that freedom, we have no grounds for complaint when he uses disguises in order to write."[25] Kauffman and Taubman's articles, despite their difference in intent, became somewhat infamous. Theatre historian Kaier Curtin notes, "Had any of the playwrights heeded Taubman and Kauffmann's advice and written about gay lifestyles in the 1960s, the subject matter would have hung about their necks like an albatross."[26] What is curiously absent from Kauffmann and Taubman's pieces is nearly any mention at all of musical theatre, apart from one swipe by Taubman at the unnamed "male designer [who] dresses the girls in a musical to make them unappealing and disrobes the boys so that more male skin is visible than art or illusion require."[27] Was musical theatre's association with male homosexuality already that much of an open secret, or were its gay creators simply able to hide behind the heterosexual visibility of industry giants like George Abbott, Richard Rodgers and Oscar Hammerstein, Bob Fosse, and Harold Prince? That there were no comparable think pieces in the *Times* speculating about how the sexuality of Cole Porter or Michael Bennett or Lorenz Hart, to name just three names, "contaminated" their work speaks to how little serious attention critics then considered musicals worthy of receiving (outside of reviews).

These articles are an inextricable part of the legacy of the *Times* and its treatment of gays in print. Journalist Joshua Keating explains that Kauffmann's "article caused controversy not for what it had to say about homosexuality, but for mentioning it at all."[28] Kauffmann's article incensed the mother of the publisher of the *Times*, Iphigene Sulzberger, and Kauffmann was no longer in his job six months later. Sulzberger intervened in the family business again in 1975 after "another article that highlighted lesbians and gays," resulting in the explicit ban of the word "gay" from the *Times* until 1987, ensured that the more-clinical sounding "homosexual" would be the word of choice for the paper throughout the final years of the gay liberation movement and the early years of AIDS.[29] The larger issue is one of visibility; political scientists Daniel Chomsky and Scott Barclay studied the coverage of lesbians and gays in the *Times* and concluded that "the *New York Times* paid virtually no attention to lesbians and gays at all," despite vast social changes since the late 1960s. In fact, "the few articles that mentioned gays in this period were strikingly hostile."[30] Notably absent from the front page of the *Times* was the founding event of the gay liberation movement: the six-night-long series of Stonewall riots.[31] The American Psychiatric Association's 1973 removal of homosexuality from the DSM-IV also did not make the front page.

Though the mainstream media did not always understand or celebrate these events or recognize their importance at the time, the world was forever changed by the end of the prior eras of repression and censorship. And theatre responded in kind, as the case studies that follow will show. If it is clear that the media colluded to closet homosexuality in the face of its growing social acceptance, it is also clear that it only mattered so much: more and more gay people began to come out, more rights were won at ballot boxes and in important court cases, and more representation ensued. Musicals responded, albeit slowly, in kind.

Reading Musicals Queerly

If it was rare to see accurate representations and understandings of queer people in the mainstream press, this lack provided a gap which scholars later gladly filled. The then-new field of queer theory coalesced in the 1980s and 1990s in response to social and state-sanctioned homophobia and emerged in tandem with contemporary social movements in queer identity politics. As queer theory became an increasingly dominant mode of inquiry in the humanities in and after the 1990s (thanks to scholars like Lauren Berlant, Leo Bersani, Judith Butler, David Halperin, Teresa de Lauretis, Eve Kosofsky Sedgwick, D. D. Miller, Adrienne Rich, and Michael Warner among too many others to name here), musical theatre studies too began to coalesce as a field (albeit on a much smaller scale). Though both fields were in some ways outsiders in the academy, queer theory gained legitimacy before musical theatre studies did. Queer theory was heady, slick, cool, and a little dangerous while musical theatre was, well, popular but decidedly not cool.

Musical theatre scholar Elizabeth L. Wollman notes in her history of the field of musical theatre studies how "the musical's uncool reputation has distanced musical theater studies from other disciplines that examine popular culture but whose objects of study are less obviously middlebrow, or at least more effective at concealing their dependence on the marketplace."[32] Musicals represent open participation in (and, to some, a capitulation to) capitalism that queer theory and radical queer politics largely challenge. Queer theory was also, crucially, framed as *theory*, while musical theatre was initially marginalized within academic fields like theatre studies and musicology as less worthy of study than the work of Shakespeare or Bach, for instance.

When English professor Scott McMillin introduced musical theatre into the curriculum at Cornell University at the turn of the twenty-first century, he challenged students, asking them "not to wonder if the musical is up to the standards of the university but if the standards of the

university are up to dealing with the musical."[33] Now that
that question has been settled to a degree (as this series you
are reading proves), musical theatre studies has a place in
the academy. The field has expanded but always circles back
to the form's long association with queerness. Many of the
first monographs published in the then-nascent field focused
squarely on queer readings of the stage musical.[34]

In 1998, Harvard University Press published noted
literary theorist D. A. Miller's *Place for Us: Essay on the
Broadway Musical*. Miller's groundbreaking book dared not
just to theorize gay male identity and its enmeshment with
musicals but to theorize musicals themselves as gay, even if
their inherent gayness was disavowed and misrecognized. He
writes, "the dilapidated form is now getting acknowledged
. . . as a somehow *gay* genre, the only one that mass culture
ever produced."[35] Miller organized his book around the
spaces in which gay boys and men immersed themselves in
musicals in the mid-to-late twentieth century (their parents'
basement, the piano bar, and the Broadway theatre), making
it at once a deeply personal treatise and a profound statement
to both the academy and to readers about the importance of
these spaces, gay men's cultural attachments, and musicals
themselves. In a much lighter vein than Miller, theatre
historian John M. Clum's *Something for the Boys: Musical
Theater and Gay Culture* (1999) offered an "autobiographical,
not sociological or anthropological" romp through his own
highly opinionated take on this special relationship.[36]

The attention paid to gay men's relationship to musicals
in the cultural imagination threatened to eclipse the fact
that other queer people beyond gay men have thoughts

and feelings about musicals too. Musical theatre scholar Stacy Wolf's *A Problem Like Maria: Gender and Sexuality in the American Musical* (2002) "is a book about musicals from a feminist, lesbian perspective."[37] Wolf's lesbian feminist readings of musicals and musical theatre stars shaped the field of musical theatre studies and modeled new ways of understanding spectatorship and new ways of looking at musicals and the marginalized people who love them. Wolf's and Miller's critically queer works were an important scholarly coming out as they staked claims about the importance of musicals. In particular, their work demonstrates the kinds of queer readings that musicals invited queer people to practice since musicals did not represent them onstage, and if they did, it was certainly not with much accuracy. Wolf's next book, *Changed for Good: A Feminist History of the Broadway Musical* (2011), extended her project of challenging musical theatre's heteronormativity by reading musicals queerly and looking at female homosocial relationships within the form.

If Wolf and Miller focused largely on positive affective readings of musicals, lesbian writer Sarah Schulman's *Stage Struck: Theater, AIDS, and the Marketing of Gay America* (1998) critically examined how mainstream theatre appropriated queer culture and forcefully argued that Jonathan Larson constructed his musical *Rent* (1996) by plagiarizing many aspects of her novel *People in Trouble* (1987). *Rent* also proved a deep disappointment to theatre scholar David Savran, who contends, "*Rent*'s exploitation of racial minorities is echoed by its exploitation of sexual minorities," going on to argue that *Rent* staged queerness only to signify "upper-middlebrow chic" in order to distinguish itself in the Broadway marketplace.[38] These arguments about *Rent* show the pitfalls of the uneasy co-existence of queer narratives in the capitalist marketplace of the commercial musical.

Miller and Wolf's work continues to shape the field; theatre scholar LaDonna L. Forsgren's important 2019 *Theatre Survey* article "*The Wiz* Redux; or, Why Queer Black Feminist Spectatorship and Politically Engaged Entertainment Continue to Matter" extends Wolf's approach to feminist spectatorship and expands the field in new directions to argue "that queer black feminist spectators might interpret Dorothy's fantasy as a black lesbian narrative" in order to theorize both how Black feminist spectatorship matters and the social responsibility of artists.[39] Following Miller's influence, musical theatre scholar Bradley Rogers finds a contradiction between musical's heteronormativity and queer attraction to the form, noting, "the musical's investment in boy-meets-girl romance—proves in fact to be paradoxically central to the queer dimensions of the genre: the musical's unique structure exacerbated the potential for queer energies to erupt in unexpected places, revealing the omnipresence of those queer energies."[40] Scholars are undertaking research on everything from queer temporality and queer representation to queer musicals in the global context as well as familiar yet evolving terrain like casting and identity.

While scholars initially looked at the Broadway musical as their object of study, Broadway wasn't the only venue of importance to queer musical theatre makers. Off-Broadway allowed more license for openness when it came to gay and lesbian representation than the commercial context and mainstream glare of Broadway audience. Indeed, "the first commercial musical in New York City devoted entirely to contemporary gay issues" was called *The Faggot* and opened in 1973 Off-Off Broadway.[41] More followed over the course of the 1970s on, Off-, and Off-Off-Broadway as Wollman details in *Hard Times: The Adult Musical in 1970s New York City* (2013). In a similar vein, Kirle looks at three musicals that played Broadway in 1970 (*Applause*, *Coco*, and *Company*) and argues that their "principal characters are sexually ambiguous, either through text, performance, or both," which presaged the sexual revolution gay liberation intended to bring about.[42] Broadway has long had a symbiotic relationship with Off-Broadway, especially when it comes to finding hit musicals and musicals with queer content.

Prime among the queer approaches in and to musical theatre of the 1970s onstage was *A Chorus Line* (1975), which began life at Off-Broadway's The Public Theater before going on to become (for a time) Broadway's longest-running musical. Because *A Chorus Line* featured several gay male characters, it has been a fecund object for scholars studying musicals and queer identity. For instance, theatre scholar Alberto Sandoval-Sánchez writes of the intersections of the character Paul's Nuyorican identity and his sexuality, "While his ethnicity is invisible in the beginning of the musical, his sexuality is always visibly inscribed on his body. His gayness, a marker of difference, makes it impossible for him to pass as a macho man, Puerto Rican or Anglo. The audience will remember most his gayness and cross-dressing experience because these have upstaged his identity."[43] As Sandoval-

Sánchez's writing demonstrates, scholarly attention was turning to how various facets of identity inform each other in performance and reception beyond the text. As scholars, we look back to understand how the past points the way forward. Understanding past shows like *The Wiz* or *A Chorus Line* or *The Faggot* harkens us to remember that queerness existed in many guises and under many names and has almost always been deeply imbricated in musical theatre history.

The case studies that follow offer four ways of approaching musical theatre with queerness foregrounded, progressing from historical context to text, production, and, finally, reception. Though they are organized in the order in which musical theatre happens, the case studies themselves are not in chronological order. Taken together, the case studies in the chapters that follow aim to give readers a holistic sense of queer approaches in and to musical theatre.

Notes

1 Harvey Fierstein and Jerry Herman, *La Cage aux Folles* (New York: Samuel French, 1984), 109.

2 In the revised 2014 edition of the libretto, librettist Harvey Fierstein updated the stage directions to read: "(**GEORGES** joins **ALBIN** and they kiss)," 97.

3 Lindsey Mantoan, "The Utopic Vision of OSF's *Oklahoma!*: Recuperative Casting Practices and Queering Early American History," *Studies in Musical Theatre* 15, no. 1 (2021): 41–56.

4   Smithsonian.com, "As an African American, LGBTQ+
    Woman, Ethel Waters Shaped U.S. Entertainment," June
    12, 2020, *Because of Her Story (The Smithsonian)*, https://
    womenshistory.si.edu/news/2020/06/african-american-lgbtq
    -woman-ethel-waters-shaped-us-entertainment.

5   Frank Rich, review of *Dance a Little Closer*, *New York Times*,
    May 12, 1983, https://www.nytimes.com/1983/05/12/theater/
    stage-lerner-musical-dance-a-little-closer.html.

6   "queer, adj.1." OED Online. March 2022. Oxford University
    Press.

7   David M. Halperin, *How to Be Gay* (Cambridge, MA: Harvard
    University Press, 2014), 450.

8   Ibid., 451.

9   Lisa Duggan, "The New Homonormativity: The Sexual Politics
    of Neoliberalism," in *Materialising Democracy: Towards a
    Revitalized Cultural Politics*, ed. R. Castronovo and D. D.
    Nelson (Durham, NC: Duke University Press, 2002), 175–94.

10 Hannah McCann and Whitney Monaghan, *Queer Theory Now:
    From Foundations to Futures* (London: Bloomsbury, 2019), 158.

11 Jenna Wortham, "When Everyone Can Be 'Queer,' is Anyone?,"
    New York Times, July 12, 2016, https://www.nytimes.com/2016
    /07/17/magazine/when-everyone-can-be-queer-is-anyone.html.

12 "New Kind of Censorship Puts Padlock on a Theatre," *New
    York Times*, March 11, 1928, 123, https://timesmachine
    .nytimes.com/timesmachine/1928/03/11/94128040.html
    ?pageNumber=123.

13 Robert Gordon, Olaf Jubin, and Millie Taylor, *British Musical
    Theatre since 1950* (London: Bloomsbury Methuen Drama,
    2016), 13.

14 Ibid.

15 Ibid., 27.

16 Ibid.

17 Bruce Kirle, *Unfinished Show Business: Broadway Musicals as Works-in-Process* (Carbondale, IL: Southern Illinois University Press, 2005), 169.

18 Jordan Schildcrout, "Drama and the New Sexualities," in *The Oxford Handbook of American Drama*, ed. Jeffrey H. Richards and Heather S. Nathans (New York: Oxford University Press, 2014), 456.

19 Kirle, *Unfinished Show Business*, 178.

20 Moss Hart, Ira Gershwin, and Kurt Weill, "Lady in the Dark," in *Great Musicals of the American Theatre*, volume 2, ed. Stanley Richards (Radnor, PA: Chilton Book Company, 1976), 103. Hart wrote *Lady in the Dark* after his own psychoanalysis, which he underwent in order to resolve his sexual ambivalence.

21 Colden Lamb, "LADY IN THE DARK Segment from MUSICAL COMEDY TONIGHT," YouTube video (12:12), January 7, 2022, https://www.youtube.com/watch?v =EuoBouVaPyQ&t=1s.

22 Howard Taubman, "Not What It Seems: Homosexual Motif Gets Heterosexual Guise," *New York Times*, November 5, 1961.

23 Howard Taubman, "Modern Primer: Helpful Hints to Tell Appearances vs. Truth," *New York Times*, April 28, 1963.

24 Stanley Kauffmann, "Homosexual Drama and Its Disguises," *New York Times*, January 23, 1966.

25 Stanley Kauffmann, "On the Acceptability of the Homosexual," *New York Times*, February 6, 1966.

26 Kaier Curtin, *"We Can Always Call Them Bulgarians": The Emergence of Lesbians and Gay Men on the American Stage* (Boston: Alyson Publications, 1987), 326.

27 Taubman, "Not What It Seems."

28 Joshua Keating, "1987: The Year The *New York Times* Discovered Gay People," *Slate*, October 11, 2013, http://www.slate.com/blogs/outward/2013/10/11/the_new_york_times _discovered_gay_people_in_1987.html.

29 Daniel Chomsky and Scott Barclay, "The Editor, the Publisher, and His Mother: The Representation of Lesbians and Gays in the *New York Times*," *Journal of Homosexuality* 60 (2013): 1392.

30 Ibid., 1393–4.

31 Ibid., 1394. The authors also detail internal censorship at the *Times* over stories that covering lesbians and gays favorably in the 1980s, as well as the absence of AIDS from the front page until 1983.

32 Elizabeth L. Wollman, "Musical Theater Studies: A Critical View of the Discipline's History in the United States and the United Kingdom," *Music Research Annual* 2 (2021): 2.

33 Scott McMillin, *The Musical as Drama* (Princeton, NJ: Princeton University Press, 2014), xi.

34 Film musicals are entirely another matter. See, for instance, Alexander Doty, "There's Something Queer Here," in *Making Things Perfectly Queer: Interpreting Mass Culture* (Minneapolis, MN: University of Minnesota Press, 1993) for an early example of a queer reading of film and TV. See also Steven Cohan, *Incongruous Entertainment: Camp, Cultural Value, and the MGM Musical* (Durham, NC: Duke University Press, 2005).

35 D. A. Miller, *Place for Us: Essay on the Broadway Musical* (Cambridge, MA: Harvard University Press, 1998), 16.

36 John Clum, *Something for the Boys: Musical Theater and Gay Culture* (New York: Palgrave, 1999), 1.

37 Stacy Wolf, *Changed for Good: A Feminist History of the Broadway Musical* (New York: Oxford University Press, 2011), vii.

38 David Savran, *A Queer Sort of Materialism: Recontextualizing American Theater* (Ann Arbor, MI: University of Michigan Press, 2003), 41.

39 La Donna L. Forsgren, "*The Wiz* Redux, or Why Queer Black Feminist Spectatorship and Politically Engaged Popular Entertainment Continue to Matter," *Theatre Survey* 60, no. 3 (2019): 326.

40 Bradley Rogers, "The Queer Pleasures of Musicals," in *The Oxford Handbook of Music and Queerness*, ed. Fred Everett Maus and Sheila Whiteley (New York: Oxford University Press, 2019), 74.

41 Elizabeth L. Wollman, *Hard Times: The Adult Musical in 1970s New York City* (New York: Oxford University Press, 2013), 52–3.

42 Kirle, *Unfinished Show Business*, 162.

43 Alberto Sandoval-Sánchez, *José, Can You See?: Latinos On and Off Broadway* (Madison, WI: The University of Wisconsin Press, 1999), 95.

1
Historical Context
AIDS

When the Covid-19 pandemic struck in 2019, some commentators noted echoes of the concurrent pandemic: HIV (human immunodeficiency virus)/AIDS (acquired immune deficiency syndrome). While Covid-19's impact on the world and on theatre was immediate and led to prolonged closure and unemployment for most working in theatre, the impact of AIDS was slower but no less devastating to theatre, artistically if not economically. The effects of AIDS still reverberate because a generation of artists and audiences was lost and because AIDS is not over. Thinking about AIDS and musicals raises many questions, among them: How do musicals and the theatre industry remember AIDS? What are the cultural politics of representing AIDS in a mainstream commercial form like the Broadway and West End Musical? Can AIDS ever be funny? If so, at whose expense is the joke? Queer theatre scholar Alisa Solomon writes that remembering AIDS means considering "what and whom, specifically, to remember; where and when to remember them; whom to address; and how; and why."[1] She notes "that by engaging in commemoration, a society is acknowledging (even if incompletely or in a deliberately distorting way) that the historical trauma occurred."[2] When musicals stage HIV/AIDS, they bring all of these questions to bear.

This chapter first offers historical context on HIV/AIDS and then acknowledges how HIV/AIDS impacted the industry offstage before charting how musicals have dealt with the HIV/AIDS crisis onstage. Musicals first treated AIDS with gravity in musicals like *Falsettos* (1992) and *Rent* (1996) but somehow AIDS became fodder for jokes (to very different ends) in musicals like *The Book of Mormon* (2011) and *A Strange Loop* (2019). In 2021, the Broadway flop *Diana* attempted to recreate Princess Diana's famous 1987 visit to an AIDS ward, explicitly engaging in the act of remembering AIDS and restaging history. In vastly different ways and at quite different times, these musicals all prod audiences to engage in remembering. Most pressingly, these artistic acts of remembering force reckoning with the fact that, as HIV/AIDS researcher Dr. Robert Grant noted in 2019, "we know how to end this epidemic. We have all the technology we need to end this epidemic, and yet we don't. We don't end this epidemic."[3]

HIV/AIDS histories often begin in 1981, the year that its spread began to make the medical establishment take notice. Scientists now estimate that HIV, the virus that causes AIDS, originated in or around 1908, meaning that HIV was spreading unchecked for many decades before it became a pandemic.[4] It typically takes a few years before HIV develops into AIDS, allowing those who have contracted HIV to unknowingly spread it while asymptomatic. HIV/

AIDS initially afflicted marginalized populations around the world and governments largely shrugged off the responsibility of responding to the growing pandemic at first. Once it became clear that HIV/AIDS did not impact only gays (and intravenous drug users) but could infect anyone, it was already too late to stop its spread. Despite the fact that gay men and women and allies in New York City and other urban centers began organizing in 1981 once it was clear that something was very wrong, there were no legal protections for people with AIDS for a very long time and so they were openly and legally discriminated against. Worse, there was no effective treatment for HIV/AIDS until the mid-1990s.

In the early years of HIV/AIDS in the 1980s, while it was not even clear how the syndrome was spread (as *Falsettos* depicts), panic and fear caused terrible shunning of gays (as *A Strange Loop* shows); people dying of AIDS were sometimes abandoned by their families (as in *Rent*'s milieu) and some nurses and caregivers refused to touch them (as *Diana* depicts). It was hard to find accurate information about HIV/AIDS at all in the early years, which was only compounded by the fact "that the *Times* downplayed the rapid and devastating spread of AIDS through the gay community in the early 1980s."[5] Media scholar Larry Gross details how a two-month-long outbreak of Legionnaire's disease led to sixty-two stories (eleven of which made the front page) in the *Times*, while "in dramatic contrast, from July 1981 through the end of 1982, the *New York Times* ran a total of ten stories about AIDS, and none of them reached the front page. The television networks did not even mention

AIDS on their nightly newscasts until 1982."[6] The media's near-silence spoke volumes.

The stigma existed at the highest levels of the US government. US president Ronald Reagan did not even publicly acknowledge HIV/AIDS until 1985, the year whose "figures showed an 89 percent increase in new AIDS cases compared with 1984."[7] In 1985, the first year testing for HIV became available, the average time from diagnosis to death was a scant fifteen months.[8] This fact is why Schulman describes "the years from 1981 to 1996" as "a mass death experience of young people."[9] In 1996 a lifesaving treatment arrived, colloquially known as the AIDS "cocktail," which made the syndrome chronic for those with access to the medication. *Rent* takes place in the years just before the cocktail was available. It was a long fifteen-year wait from 1981 to 1996, and an even longer wait if you were not a white gay man in the United States with access or health care.

Because HIV/AIDS initially spread widely and silently among gay and bisexual men, the theatre was especially impacted since it was one of few industries where gay men could live openly (if still closeted outside of work). Not only boldface names like director-choreographer Michael Bennett (*A Chorus Line*) and choreographer Michael Peters (*Dreamgirls*) were lost to AIDS, but numerous chorus dancers, stage managers, box office personnel, marketing associates, wardrobe stylists, casting personnel—in short, not a single facet of theatre was untouched. The theatre industry organized charities like Broadway Cares/Equity Fights AIDS in the United States, and the Make a Difference Trust and West End Cares in the United Kingdom to raise awareness and funds for people with HIV/AIDS and for HIV/AIDS research. Through fundraisers and benefit performances, these organizations stepped in when governmental and social support structures did not. Onstage in the 1990s, musicals began to catch up to plays like *Angels in America* (1991) and *The Normal Heart* (1985) and their representations of AIDS.

Despite *Rent*'s insistence on people "living with, not dying from disease," Broadway musicals staged the opposite by showing audiences characters both living with *and* dying of HIV/AIDS—and this was a political act. In the 1990s, while AIDS was a leading killer of adults in the United States, two musicals addressed the pandemic head-on as central elements of their narrative: *Falsettos* and *Rent*. That these musicals appeared on Broadway at all at the time just before the dominance of corporate producers like Disney Theatricals profoundly shifted paradigms of Broadway aesthetics and economics remains surprising; that both came to Broadway from developmental runs at nonprofit Off-Broadway institutional theatres was less so. Risks were easier to take Off-Broadway, where less money was at stake. Since most Broadway shows fail to return their investments, it is remarkable that producers took risks on musicals that made AIDS central. Yet to ignore HIV/AIDS and its impact would have also been perilous.

Falsettos was the first Broadway musical after *La Cage aux Folles* with a gay male love story at its center. Unlike its predecessor, which openly sought to entertain mainstream audiences with its gaudy costumes and mid-century musical comedy form, *Falsettos* was contemporary in look and form. The original production ran for over 400 performances and a

2016 revival brought the show to new audiences on Broadway and on tour across the country. The show, by composer-lyricist William Finn, was the combination of characters and elements largely from the final two musicals in Finn's Off-Broadway trilogy, comprised of *In Trousers* (1979), *March of the Falsettos* (1981), and *Falsettoland* (1990), about the irascibly neurotic-yet-lovable Marvin, his lover, his ex-wife, and their son. It's a complicated, funny, wry examination of a seemingly heteronormative Jewish nuclear family whose lives get profoundly changed when Marvin, the father, comes out and finds a male lover, Whizzer.

Though the first two shows in the "Marvin trilogy" did not address HIV/AIDS due to the fact that it hadn't yet been identified, *Falsettoland* could not avoid it and depicting its devastating impact. *Falsettoland* later became the second act of *Falsettos*. The first act opens with "Four Jews in a Room Bitching," which sets the tone of the show, announces its themes, and introduces its characters. *Falsettos* is funny, at least in Act One, with songs like "I'm Breaking Down" and "My Father's a Homo." Things darken in the second act, set in 1981. Marvin and Whizzer's neighbors, a lesbian couple named Charlotte and Cordelia, enter the story.[10] Charlotte is a doctor increasingly alarmed at the number of gay men coming into the hospital with an unknown illness, which she sings about in "Something Bad Is Happening." She explains, "Bachelors arrive sick and frightened/They leave weeks later unenlightened/We see a trend/But the trend has no name."[11] Whizzer falls ill with the mystery illness, which audiences will recognize as HIV/AIDS but the characters cannot know as such yet. The final scenes take place in Whizzer's hospital room. Whizzer dies a few songs later (*Falsettos* is largely sung-through, though there is dialogue by James Lapine), just after singing a tour-de-force number called "You Gotta Die Sometime." His ghost reappears in the show's emotional peak, singing "What Would I Do?" with Marvin. Marvin asks Whizzer, "Who would I be if I had not loved you?"[12]

If the choice to include HIV/AIDS in the narrative was really no choice at all—a contemporary musical about gay life in New York City in the 1980s had to include it—then the issue became how to do so. Finn noted, "I can't have AIDS be peripheral in the show, and I don't know that I could write about AIDS head-on because the horror is too real and I don't want to trivialize it."[13] In the end, *Falsettos* confronted HIV/AIDS and made the characters' growing sense of dread and grief quite real, underlining the show's emotional impact. It is crucial to remember that *Falsettos* initially opened when AIDS was still a terminal illness with no effective treatments; by the time of its 2016 Broadway revival, treatments had made HIV chronic and preventable, making *Falsettos* something of a time capsule as well as an educational experience for young people. Lapine noted that AIDS "pretty much decimated the artistic community, which was hit very hard by it. I think it's interesting that a lot of young gay people don't realize the importance of that here in that period. It's interesting for them to have a sense of the reality of it."[14] And it was important that Whizzer, probably the most beloved character in the musical, was the one to die. AIDS deaths did not follow any rhyme or reason; it is an unpredictable killer and why some people are spared and others are not remains a conundrum. *Falsettos* moved audiences touched by HIV/AIDS as well as those who were perhaps not yet directly affected and proved that musicals could stage contemporary gay and lesbian life while succeeding commercially and artistically. As earlier groundbreaking musicals had done before it, *Falsettos* proved again that musicals did not only have to be escapist or have happy endings in order to find audiences.

If *Falsettos* was an unlikely Broadway hit, *Rent* was an incontrovertible smash, winning many prizes, enjoying a twelve-year Broadway run, spawning a film adaptation, a live television version, and hundreds of productions around the world. *Rent*'s legend was cemented when its creator Jonathan Larson died at thirty-five the day before his show was set to begin performances at Off-Broadway's New York Theatre Workshop. The show's impact, though, was due to its content, which was much queerer than the typical musical then, and its form: the rock musical. *Rent* queered the musical by having its straight romantic leading couple both be HIV+ and by making its two secondary couples queer (and one of these couples, Angel and Collins, was HIV+). *Rent* also queered opera since it is ostensibly a resetting of Puccini's *La Bohème* to New York's East Village, a neighborhood seemingly always rapidly gentrifying. (In a meta-twist that makes the musical very "New York," in one light, *Rent* depicts gentrifiers complaining about gentrification.) Though I and others have elsewhere held *Rent* to account for its representations of HIV/AIDS, I will focus here on aspects of the show that are affirmative.[15]

Despite the tropes around HIV/AIDS that *Rent* embodies (only the queer, gender nonconforming HIV+ character dies while the heterosexual leads live), it powerfully expressed the ethics of care and community that surrounded many people with HIV/AIDS in the 1980s and 1990s, often in the absence of their nuclear families. In the first act, the song "Life Support" takes place at a support group of the same name where participants sing the mantra, "No day but today." (This lyric went on to become the show's marketing tagline, showing that *Rent*'s producers did not necessarily shy away from the show's HIV/AIDS content.) A supporting character, Gordon, chafes at the relentless positivity of the mantra and confronts the Life Support leader, saying, "My t-cells are low. I regret that news."[16] The moment is short but powerful. Roger, the show's leading man, and the members of Life Support later reappear to sing "Will I?" about their fears of dying of AIDS. HIV/AIDS appears again when an alarm goes off in the transition between the penultimate songs of the first act, "La Vie Boheme" and "I Should Tell You." This moment shows all four HIV+ characters (Angel, Collins, Mimi, and Roger) taking an "AZT break" as they all pop the pills that were the only available but not wholly effective HIV/AIDS treatment in the early 1990s. The cast says in unison at one point, "Act up—fight AIDS," the well-worn chant of HIV/AIDS activist group ACT UP.

It is important to note that none of the HIV+ characters are shunned because of their HIV status or their sexuality; all are welcomed into the community of the musical. They are not *othered* because they have HIV/AIDS; rather, they are centered. Even though the ensemble memorably sings, "to people living with/living with/living with not dying from disease," at the end of Act One, AIDS almost always foreshadowed death in theatre then: Once a show introduced someone with HIV/AIDS, you could safely bet they would die before the curtain fell. *Rent*'s emotional peak comes in the middle of the second act when Angel dies and Collins movingly eulogizes her death in "I'll Cover You (Reprise)." All of this queer content was revolutionary for a mainstream Broadway musical, and the cast was racially and ethnically diverse to boot. That *Rent* lasted on Broadway for more than a decade speaks to the fact that Broadway musical audiences were ready for queer content and plots that dealt with HIV/AIDS. Indeed, *Rent* filled the gap left behind when *Falsettos* closed. Writer Bob Ickes noted in *Poz* magazine (the US monthly for people with and affected by HIV/AIDS) that upon *Rent*'s Broadway closing, "When *Rent*'s final curtain closes, HIV will be absent from the Great White Way." He went on to ask, "In a sanitized, Disney-zed Broadway world of little mermaids, where a spoonful of sugar helps our AIDS meds go down, where are the artists challenging and educating a modern audience about the villain virus that refuses to die?"[17] The answer came not in the form of a challenge or a lesson but as a joke.

Three years after *Rent*'s closing, HIV/AIDS would return to Broadway musicals via a most unlikely source: *The Book of Mormon*. The tragedy of HIV/AIDS makes it a subversive yet obvious target for satire and dark humor and two musicals after *Rent* which would target the issue in just that way—with wildly different means and vastly different ends—are *Mormon* and *A Strange Loop*. Both musicals connected HIV/AIDS to Blackness, with the former presenting a disingenuously racist, colonial view of Black Africans and the latter using sharp-edged humor to critique homophobia. *Mormon*'s irreverence heralds the signature tone of its libertarian, contrarian writers: *South Park* creators Matt Parker and Try Stone and songwriter Robert Lopez (*Frozen*, *Avenue Q*). *Mormon* is set in a village in Uganda, where two Mormon missionaries arrive to try and convert the locals to their religion. *Mormon*'s Ugandans are beset both by HIV/AIDS and ignorance about its transmission; some of the fictionalized Ugandans in the show believe that HIV/AIDS can be cured by sex with a virgin, which leads them to raping babies when few virgins remain.[18] This is all meant to be outré humor that pushes the limits, yet given the very real toll that AIDS has taken on the entire African continent, "how funny can it be that AIDS has ravaged Africa?"[19]

A Strange Loop takes a completely dissimilar tack in its approach to AIDS, an approach that is deadly serious even while it has the audacity to imagine a Tyler Perry-esque gospel play-within-the-play, unforgettably musicalized in the song "AIDS Is God's Punishment." Unlike *Mormon*, *Loop* marks a return (in Broadway musicals, at least) to taking AIDS seriously but with a lacerating sense of humor. *Loop* creator Michael R. Jackson (book, music, and lyrics) dedicated the musical to "all those Black gay boys I knew who chose to go on back to the Lord," a reference to those who have died of AIDS. In "AIDS Is God's Punishment," Jackson takes aim at homophobia, specifically from the church pulpit, rather than at people with AIDS (á la *Mormon*). The number comes after Usher, the protagonist, has a fight with his homophobic mother, who has repeatedly asked him to write a Tyler Perry-style gospel play. Usher begins the song "in honor of Brother Darnell, who was an abomination just like me" and notes that he was told at church "the only thing worse than dying of AIDS was living with it."[20] The song is a pseudo-sermon in which the title is repeated over and over to hammer home the homophobia with which Usher's church and family attempted to indoctrinate him. No Broadway musical before dared address homophobia so directly nor had any directly confronted in one fell swoop the intersections of anti-Blackness, AIDS stigma, homophobia, and Christianity, not to mention sizeism. *Loop* represents a paradigm shift in queer approaches in musical theatre. This "Pulitzer Prize-winning big, Black, and queer American musical" (as the show's marketing tagline proudly announces) takes musicals to places they've never been, with bodies usually sidelined taking center stage. Unapologetically Black, fat, and queer, *A Strange Loop*'s success represents a more inclusive queerness in musicals. These contrasting examples show that it is not the case that humor and AIDS are incompatible, but rather that the target of the joke—and who is making it—matters.

If all of the aforementioned shows presented fictional characters, three musicals attempted to dramatize the impact of AIDS on historical subjects. Two of these began life beyond Broadway and the West End, *Taboo* (2002) and *The Boy from Oz* (1998), and focused respectively on British performance artist Leigh Bowery and Australian singer-songwriter Peter Allen. The third, *Diana: The Musical*, fictionalized historical events like Princess Diana's visits to

HIV/AIDS wards in hospitals in the 1980s. All three musicals acknowledge the deaths HIV/AIDS caused. Leigh Bowery is memorialized in *Taboo*'s poignant "Il Adore," which takes place in the hospital room where he is dying a lonely death (in contrast to how Whizzer dies in *Falsettos*). In *Oz*, Allen and his lover both succumb to AIDS before the curtain falls and another of Allen's pop songs blares away. *Diana* stages its title character's visit to an AIDS ward, before which her husband Prince Charles begs her not to, but says if she must go, to "protect" herself and "wear gloves, wear a mask." Diana responds, "AIDS is a growing crisis in Britain and no one is paying the least bit of attention to it." She refuses the gloves and walks in to see the patients, who have been instructed not to touch her, and she grasps their hands. Though *Diana* was unintentionally campy much of the time, it did treat its HIV/AIDS scene with dignity, raising awareness of the stigma directed at people with HIV/AIDS and how Princess Diana directly and cannily combated that stigma with a photo opportunity (in the song "Secrets and Lies").[21] It was a rare genuine moment in an otherwise tabloid-level take on Princess Diana's life as a royal. By drawing directly on a global event—Princess Diana's historic humanizing of people with HIV/AIDS—*Diana* prompts consideration of how musicals can remember HIV/AIDS at a time when it might seem like part of the distant past to those not alive in the 1980s.

Solomon's article "What does it mean to remember AIDS?" poses a central question that these musicals raise: What of the fact that some of them were written by survivors?[22] The musicals themselves are ways of grappling with the parallel legacies of HIV/AIDS *and* of HIV/AIDS representations. When older shows are revived, they risk feeling archival and didactic, but when they aren't revived there is the danger that HIV/AIDS may be forgotten. Yet if the public has largely turned their attention away from HIV/AIDS, it is still here. And work about HIV/AIDS remains contemporary and relevant, as *A Strange Loop* proves. Musicals can help process the trauma, whose effects have larger implications. Schulman explains: "The trauma of AIDS—a trauma that has yet to be defined or understood, for which no one has been made accountable—has produced a gentrification of the mind for gay people. We have been streamlining into a highly gendered, privatized family/marriage structure en masse."[23] Yet not all HIV/AIDS representations accede to the gentrified structures Schulman laments, even in the commercialized form of the Broadway musical. For instance, *Taboo*, like *Loop* after it, was openly queer in its marketing.[24] The fact that it was a commercial flop on Broadway perhaps speaks as much to its artistic failures as to its in-your-face queerness—what other Broadway show's marketing campaign featured a man cruising for sex at a urinal?

Remembering HIV/AIDS in musicals proves that they still contain the power to disturb. *Rent* could unsettle homophobes even in 2022, when a theatregoer in Leeds, England reportedly walked out of the show because, in their words, "I didn't realise this show was about gays."[25] These kinds of incidents remind us that homophobia and AIDS stigma have not disappeared just because social progress has been won, yet also that musicals are a profoundly affective form through which to remember.

Solomon describes how visual artist Deb Kass created two paintings for her *Feel Good Paintings for Feel Bad Times* series that reference the Sondheim musicals *Company* and *Follies*. One features the words "Being Alive" in front of a hyper-color background, while the other features the words "Still Here" in the foreground before four stripes of various colors and widths. Notably absent from the latter is the subject and verb: "I'm."[26] This absence stands in for those lost to AIDS as well as represents the survivors who are still here: as Solomon notes, "Yes, some of us are. And so is AIDS."[27] Remembering AIDS in song and dance means feeling the absence created by loss (being "still here") and also feeling the joys of "being alive." If musicals impart an array of emotions when they stage HIV/AIDS, from numbness to pain, anger, and fear, then these feelings could prompt reflection on the fact that HIV/AIDS has never ended. HIV/AIDS representations created at different times engage audiences in a comparative act of remembering—what was it like then and what is it like now? What has changed? Why is AIDS ongoing? Why do many audiences around the world take *Mormon*'s mocking representation at face value? Why has a pathbreaking musical like *Rent* seen "its status as an important piece of art [devolve] from musical wunderkind to frequent punchline" and "regarded more as a relic?"[28] Is art about AIDS now passé to younger generations never taught about it? Where would queerness and musical theatre be if HIV/AIDS had never happened? And also, to paraphrase *Falsettos'* Marvin, who would we be if we had not loved people with HIV/AIDS?

Notes

1   Alisa Solomon, "What Does It Mean to Remember AIDS?,"
    Nation, November 30, 2017, https://www.thenation.com/
    article/archive/what-does-it-mean-to-remember-aids/.

2   Ibid.

3   Michael Barbaro, "This Drug Could End H.I.V. Why Hasn't
    It," June 5, 2019, in *The Daily*, produced by *New York Times*,
    podcast, 29:42, https://www.nytimes.com/2019/06/05/
    podcasts/the-daily/hiv-aids-truvada-prep.html.

4   "HIV Has Been in Humans for 100 Years, Study Says," *New
    York Times*, October 1, 2008, https://www.nytimes.com/2008
    /10/01/world/europe/01iht-aids.1.16608463.html.

5   Daniel Chomsky and Scott Barclay, "The Editor, the Publisher,
    and His Mother: The Representation of Lesbians and Gays
    in the *New York Times*," *Journal of Homosexuality* 60 (2013):
    1400.

6   Larry Gross, *Up from Invisibility: Lesbians, Gay Men, and the
    Media in America* (New York: Columbia University Press,
    2001), 96.

7   Boyce Rensberger, "AIDS Cases in 1985 Exceed Total of All
    Previous Years," *Washington Post*, January 17, 1986, https://
    www.washingtonpost.com/archive/politics/1986/01/17/aids
    -cases-in-1985-exceed-total-of-all-previous-years/38c933d7
    -260c-414b-80f7-0dd282415cc6/.

8   Ibid.

9   Sarah Schulman, *The Gentrification of the Mind* (Berkeley, CA:
    University of California Press, 2012), 45.

10 Charlotte and Cordelia go unnamed onstage but their names
    appear in the libretto and the playbill.

11 2016 Broadway Revival Cast, "Something Bad Is Happening/ More Racquetball," disc 2, track 8 on *Falsettos* (2016 Broadway Cast Recording), 2016, Sh-K-Boom Records, Inc. and Lincoln Center Theater, streaming.

12 2016 Broadway Revival Cast, "What Would I Do?," disc 2, track 17 on *Falsettos* (2016 Broadway Cast Recording).

13 William Finn, interview with Linda Buchwald, *The Times of Israel*, December 12, 2016, https://www.timesofisrael.com/the -jewish-story-behind-the-broadway-hit-falsettos/.

14 Tracy E. Gilchrist, "*Falsettos*' Story of Love & Family Amid the Onset of AIDS Is Timeless," *Advocate*, April 2, 2019, https://www.advocate.com/theater/2019/4/02/falsettos-story -love-family-amid-onset-aids-timeless.

15 See Ryan Donovan, *Broadway Bodies: A Critical History of Conformity* (New York: Oxford University Press, 2023); Sarah Schulman, *Stagestruck: Theater, AIDS, and the Marketing of Gay America* (Durham, NC: Duke University Press, 1998); David Savran, "*Rent*'s Due: Multiculturalism and the Spectacle of Difference," *Journal of American Drama and Theatre* 14, no. 1 (2002): 1–14.

16 Original Broadway Cast "Rent," "Life Support," track 6 on *The Best of Rent*, 1999, SKG Music, LLC, streaming.

17 Bob Ickes, "Rent Decrease," *Poz*, October 1, 2008, https://www .poz.com/article/rent-broadway-hiv-15305-8144.

18 Original Broadway Cast, "Hasa Diga Eebowai," track 4 on *The Book of Mormon* (Original Broadway Cast Recording), 2011, Ghost Light Records, streaming.

19 Janice C. Simpson, "The Root: Is Broadway's 'Book of Mormon' Offensive?" *NPR*, April 15, 2011, https://www.npr .org/2011/04/15/135437800/the-root-is-broadways-book-of -mormon-offensive.

20   Original Cast, "Precious Little Dream/AIDS Is God's
     Punishment," track 15 on *A Strange Loop* Original Cast
     Recording, 2019, Yellow Sound Label, streaming.

21   *Diana the Musical*, directed by Christopher Ashley (2021, Los
     Gatos, CA: Netflix), streaming.

22   Solomon, "What Does It Mean?"

23   Schulman, *Gentrification*, 155.

24   See Ryan Donovan, "If You Were Gay, That'd Be Okay:
     Marketing LGBTQ Musicals from *La Cage* to *The Prom*,"
     in *Gender, Sex and Sexuality in Musical Theatre: He/She/
     They Could Have Dance All Night*, ed. Kelly Kessler (Bristol:
     Intellect, 2022).

25   Matt Keeley, "Theatergoer Walked Out of 'Rent' Because the
     'Show Was About Gays,'" *Newsweek*, March 14, 2022, https://
     www.newsweek.com/theatergoer-walked-out-rent-because
     -show-was-about-gays-1687962.

26   Deborah Kass, "Feel Good Paintings for Feel Bad Times," n.d.,
     https://deborahkass.com/feel-good-paintings.html.

27   Solomon, "What Does It Mean?"

28   Caroline Franke, "Why *Rent* Feels so Outdated 20 Years After
     Its Debut," *Vox*, April 29, 2016, https://www.vox.com/2016/4
     /29/11531350/rent-musical-20th-anniv/ersary.

2
Text
Fun Home

Fun Home (2015) is a radically queer musical in content and form, and also in its very existence given the musical's gay male-centric focus. *Fun Home* is the rare musical that centers a lesbian protagonist. Up to *Fun Home*'s Broadway debut, there had been so little lesbian representation in Broadway and West End musicals as to be negligible. The unnamed lesbians next door in *Falsettos* and *Rent*'s secondary couple, Maureen and Joanne, represented the musical's most prominent (though not only) lesbians up to that time. *The Color Purple* (2005) followed, and while its protagonist, Celie, sang openly of her love for the sexpot singer Shug Avery, she never comes out or even appears to struggle to accept her sexuality in the ways that *Fun Home* would later dramatize, which speaks to how the characters inhabiting the world of *The Color Purple* may have felt as much to the fact that the year if its debut, 2005, was quite a different time than when *Fun Home* opened in 2015. What is clear is that *Fun Home* did not shy away from its subject matter.[1]

Fun Home dares to look back at cartoonist Alison Bechdel's complicated family history as well as how the past is in the present, queering the musical's relationship to space and time as well as the content and form of musical theatre dramaturgy. Performance scholar Jaclyn Pyror sums it up: "[I]t's also a play about time and time travel, history and memory, and the ways in which stories get constructed, represented, rearranged, and retold."[2] If this musical is clearly queer in its content, then how does it queer the form of the book musical? In this case study on the text of a musical, I'll begin by examining the *Fun Home*'s content, then its form, its performance as text, and untangle how all of these contribute to its meanings.

Fun Home is a book musical by Lisa Kron (book and lyrics) and Jeanine Tesori (music), adapted from Bechdel's groundbreaking 2006 graphic memoir of the same name. The memoir is a look back at her youth and her family history from the vantage of middle age. If Bechdel's place in queer culture was assured thanks to her comic strip *Dykes to Watch Out For* (1983–2008), *Fun Home* cemented it and broadened her readership. Kron was an established playwright and performer in New York City by the time she and Tesori began their collaboration, which was Kron's first musical. She had previously made her Broadway debut as the star and playwright of *Well* (2006) after first gaining acclaim as a member of theatre company The Five Lesbian Brothers, in the 1980s and 1990s. Tesori brought Broadway musical bona fides to the adaptation, having written several musicals up to this point including *Violet* (1997), *Caroline, or Change* (2004), and *Shrek the Musical* (2008). In 2015, Kron and Tesori's work on *Fun Home* made them the first female writing team to win the Tony Award for Best Original Score.

Kron and Tesori worked on the show for six years before its Off-Broadway opening at The Public Theater in 2013. The challenge of adapting a graphic memoir in cartoon format into a musical was vast. Kron explained, "We created at least three-quarters of what happens in the show, if not more. There are no scenes in the book. There are no scenes! There is no dramatic action, there are no sustained scenes. There aren't even really characters."[3] On top of that was the fact that Alison appears at various ages throughout. Kron and Tesori solved the unique challenge posed by having the show's protagonist age throughout the narrative by splitting the character into three ages: Alison, Medium Alison, and Small Alison, each of whom is played by a different actor. Kron described this decision, saying, "I pretty immediately had the idea for the three Alisons. Nothing else was easy. Nothing."[4] The action of the musical occurs in Alison's memory, as she looks back at Small and Medium versions of herself and moments in her family's history that led to its unraveling. Its content is distinctively bound to its form and its graphic novel source material. And it posed unique challenges for adaptation, since, as Kron relates, "Books look backward. Theater *moves* forward." Additionally, there's the fact that "Alison is doing two things. She's remembering and she's drawing, and neither one of these things can be dramatized. They are internal."[5] Kron and Tesori had to decide how to shape the musical and what to include and to exclude from the memoir.

In terms of its content, *Fun Home* challenges musical theatre's typical heteronormativity, which was often created and enforced by closeted gay men as often as it was by heterosexuals because during the so-called Golden Age of mid-century US musical theatre openly gay or lesbian characters were an impossibility. Stacy Wolf argues, "Indeed, the ideological project of musical theatre in the mid-twentieth century United States was to use the heterosexual couple's journey from enemies to lovers to stand in for the unification of problematic differences in American culture—between the city and the country, between work and leisure, between us and them, between whites and racialized Others."[6] *Fun Home*, which ends not in a heterosexual marriage plot resolution but with the suicide of a gay man who happens to be the protagonist's father, necessarily forged its own path. If anything, the fracturing of the Bechdel family can be read as a metaphor for the broader collapse of the nuclear family at the end of the twentieth century; this musical is more about disjunction than it is about union.

The musical opens with Alison coming to her drawing table, and sitting down to draw. The audience is to understand that what she is drawing are the scenes they are seeing, which she underlines by beginning many of her lines saying "Caption" before going on to describe a feeling or an action. Small Alison enters next and sings the show's first words, "Daddy, hey Daddy, come here, okay? I need you."[7] These lyrics foreshadow the show's central conflict—the effects of Bruce Bechdel's absence, both as a parent and spouse. At the end of the opening musical sequence, "It All Comes Back

(Opening)" and "Welcome to Our House on Maple Avenue," Alison says:

> Caption: My Dad and I both grew up in the same small
>   Pennsylvania town
> And he was gay.
> And I was gay.
> And he killed himself.
> And I . . . became a lesbian cartoonist.[8]

The stakes are paradoxically raised by revealing the end at the outset. The audience knows now that part of the rest of the musical will be spent attempting to disentangle the connections Alison has just made.

Along the way, we learn that Alison grew up in the family business, a funeral home—the "fun home" alluded to in the show's ironic title—which she and her younger brothers satirize in "Come to the Fun Home," their imagined commercial for the business. Bruce also taught English at the local high school in addition to being a funeral director. Alison's mother Helen is an amateur pianist and actor in local theatre. We begin to suspect something is amiss in the Bechdel home when Bruce's former student Roy appears to help him out around the property. Kron's stage directions indicate that when introducing Helen to Roy, Bruce "puts his hand on her shoulder in a gesture that only he and Helen notice is awkward."[9] We sense that there is much that goes unsaid in the Bechdel house—and that Bruce's sexuality is more complicated than it seems at first glance, so when he and Roy are alone and he begins to seduce him by giving him sherry and telling him to unbutton his shirt, it is unsettling.

The scene then jumps ahead in time to Medium Alison coming out at college and eventually falling in love with Joan ("Changing My Major"). The show flashes back in time to Small Alison working on a school assignment to draw a map of places her family has been. Bruce, ever the perfectionist, takes it out of her hands and tells her everything she's done wrong. Alison steps in, takes the drawing, and sings "Maps." In the song, she summarizes her attraction to maps, which "show you what is simple and true."[10] In the following scene, we learn that the family troubles are worse than has been yet revealed and that Bruce has been compelled to see a psychiatrist. When Small Alison asks him why, he responds, "Because I do dumb dangerous things. Because I'm bad. Not good like you."[11] Helen tells Small Alison that this is court-ordered therapy but does not say why a judge has commanded Bruce to go. When a heated argument between Helen and Bruce ensues, Small Alison escapes into her imagination as she and her brothers sing "Raincoat of Love," a pastiche of 1970s television pop group the Partridge Family. The song concludes with Bruce maniacally singing the refrain, "Everything's alright" three times, more chillingly with each repetition.

The musical is laced through with brief epistolary scenes, where usually Bruce or Medium Alison reads a letter from or to the other. Medium Alison comes out to her parents in a letter, which they don't respond to initially, since unbeknown to her, their marriage is crumbling because of Bruce's behavior. Bruce's reply does not satisfy Medium Alison, who finds the tone insulting. The show's next two songs explore recognition and revelation. "Ring of Keys" is an iconic moment from the musical when Small Alison sees a butch lesbian delivery woman enter the diner where she and Bruce are eating. She is mesmerized by the details of the delivery woman's look, which she catalogues in the song's refrain:

> Your swagger and your bearing
> And the just-right clothes you're wearing
> Your short hair and your dungarees and your lace up
>   boots
> And your keys, oh, your ring of keys[12]

The song concludes and the scene shifts to a phone call between Medium Alison and her parents. When Helen is alone on the phone with Medium Alison, she explains her reticence to accept her daughter's sexuality right away, saying, "Alison, your father has had affairs with men."[13] This revelation (and those that follow) shake Alison to the core—the things she thought she knew turned out not to be so black and white. Bruce's mental health deteriorates as he and Helen argue incessantly. Alison notes the juxtaposition of her coming out with her father's, observing, "I didn't know, Dad, I had no way of knowing that my beginning would be your end."[14] When Medium Alison brings Joan home to meet her parents, Helen takes Medium Alison aside and tells her the truth about her marriage ("Days and Days"). After this moment, the show has only one place left to go: Bruce's suicide.

Bruce invites Medium Alison to go for a ride, leaving Joan and Helen alone. Suddenly, Alison steps effortlessly into the action for the first time, breaking memory's boundary. They drive in awkward silence ("Telephone Wire"). Bruce and Alison haltingly try to connect over their shared queerness, but Bruce gets lost in his own reverie of a college lover named Norris Jones. Bruce begins several letters to Alison but instead is having a musical breakdown ("Edges of the World") that ends with him standing in the path of oncoming headlights. Alison is left alone with her drawings, no captions coming to her mind to make sense of the senseless. The musical concludes with Small and Medium Alison joining Alison onstage ("Flying Away"), singing fragments of their respective musical themes heard earlier in the show. These themes coalesce in the lyrics, "And now I'm flying away."[15] The final line of the show is Alison's: "Caption: Every so often there was a rare moment of perfect balance when I soared above him."[16] Blackout.

If it is obvious that *Fun Home*'s content was queer, it is worth considering how its form reflected this as well. In his published collection of lyrics, Stephen Sondheim famously wrote, "content dictates form."[17] How, then, did *Fun Home*'s content dictate its form? *Fun Home* might best be described as a memory musical for the ways that it could be viewed as queering time—multiple pasts and the present occur alongside each other and sometimes happen simultaneously (and in this sense, it appears indebted in part to how Arthur Miller's 1949 play *Death of a Salesman* plays with multiple registers of time happening simultaneously). This queering is necessitated by the fact that the action audiences see onstage is happening in Alison's mind, making it quite literally a memory musical. Adding further layers to the loop of memory and time in

Fun Home, is the sense that "the past always understands itself to be the present," Lisa Kron notes in her foreword to the acting edition of the libretto.[18] The musical's sense of multiple, parallel temporalities is drawn from Bechdel's graphic novel, in which the reader is at once drawn into Bechdel's narration of her past.

Onstage, this duality was embodied in Alison, whose presence offers a key to understanding *Fun Home*'s formal queerness. Kron warns:

> It is very important that adult Alison not be misconstrued to be a narrator. She is not talking to the audience. She is not telling us things. She is a character, doggedly pursuing a goal. She is actively combing through her past, determined to piece together a truer version of her father's life than the one she's hung onto since he died. She is working—sketching, drafting, trying out ideas, trying out captions, rejecting them, refining them, and reshaping them as new information comes in. When she begins, this work is an intellectual and artistic quest.[19]

This description explains exactly how *Fun Home*'s content determined its form: Alison's search for answers meant Kron and Tesori searched for them, too. And though the musical informs audiences very early on that Bruce killed himself, spurring Alison's quest for understanding, it was crucial to its creators to preserve "the past's innocence of the future" that "makes this musical cohere and come alive."[20] Watching the multiple innocent pasts barreling toward a future that we in the audience know but the characters do not and cannot provoked an almost unbearable tension and poignancy—

it was a theatrically effective coup made possible by the show's prismatic form. Kron noted that "characters in the theater, the way they work, is that the audience has to know more about them than they know about themselves."[21] And this gap in the characters' knowledge is how the content and form of a musical, especially one as adventurous as *Fun Home*, meet to produce their intended effects upon audiences.

Musically and dramatically how did this gap function? In part, as I noted earlier, it is the fact that adult Alison tells audiences right away what the musical's denouement will be but leaves them wondering how the show will get there and what will happen along the way. Small Alison, Medium Alison, and the rest of the Bechdel family members, of course, have no clue about what's going to happen and therein lies the dramatic tension. Musicals amplify the dramatic tension in song and dance. And, as scholar Scott McMillin argues, the alternation between the drama of the book and the drama of the musical numbers is how content and form cohere to profound effect. He writes, "That is what gives the musical its lift, its energy, its elation."[22] *Fun Home* further amplifies the alternation central to musical theatre's formal nature because it alternates between the three Alisons in addition to alternating between book and song. *Fun Home* queers musical theatre dramaturgy. As McMillin argues, "In saying there are multiple selves projected by the singers and dancers, so that their characters are more than single personages, I mean that these people have the power to exceed their ordinary selves and cannot be pinned down. The deeper feelings are coming to the surface."[23] Song expands, or as McMillin would argue, "doubles" character and brings it into a new dimension of time. Yet *Fun Home* *triples* character. Because *Fun Home* also occurs in adult Alison's memory and therefore is subjective, personal, and always shifting, its sense of temporality is queer. Musical theatre scholar Sarah Whitfield suggests that "queer temporality shapes the unfolding of narrative and resolution of the story and may even deny the expected resolution that a musical usually brings."[24] Since Bruce Bechdel's suicide is both the denouement and the climax of this musical, *Fun Home* already challenges any sense of resolution with its nonlinear structure.

Musically, Tesori reinforces the destabilizing nature of adult Alison's search through her past in what Whitfield aptly describes as "consistent use of looping musical motifs which challenges the traditional expectations of how a song works in the musical: instead of reprises of whole songs, phrases and sections communicate the fragments of memory."[25] Naturally, the musical ends with a mélange of motifs heard earlier in the show. The final two tracks on the original Broadway cast album evince this. Track 26, "This Is What I Have of You . . .," demonstrates how thoroughly interwoven music and spoken text are in *Fun Home* and how the motifs recur again and again. This scene opens with the very same ostinato (a repeated musical phrase) that is the very first thing audiences hear when the musical opens—tellingly, the song is titled "It All Comes Back." At the end of the musical, it will provide the bridge between Bruce's breakdown/suicide and the finale in which all three Alisons converge and reprise parts of songs from earlier.

Alison must grapple with what to draw next and how to make sense of what she has drawn—that is, how her memories dramatized in the musical's earlier action determine what follows. She picks up a pile of drawings of her dad, saying "*This* is what I have of you" before listing what they contain.[26] She begins to draw (and speak aloud) the opening scene of the musical, depicting Small Alison:

> Daddy (comma) hey Daddy
> come here okay (question mark)
> I need // you[27]

Suddenly Small Alison actually enters and sings this phrase and then Medium Alison enters and sings a phrase from "Telephone Wire," which adult Alison sang in the scene just before Bruce's musical breakdown. The fragments overlap as time and memory collapse upon themselves before resolving into a new, major key twist on the themes in "Flying Away," which all three Alisons sing together for a moment. Kron's lyrics underline the show's central relationships, between Alison and Bruce and Alison and her past, when Alison sings "Don't let go yet."[28] The lyrics about flying away underline Alison's internal tug of war between staying tethered to her past and soaring above it.

The fact that all three Alisons sing together and that the opening ostinato recurs so many times in the musical are not accidental—very little that makes it into a musical is accidental. Who sings which songs and phrases matters because it tells the audience something about the characters, the scene, and the voice of the musical. The difference between the Bechdel family singing "Welcome to Our House on Maple Avenue" in a round and Medium Alison's waltz "Changing My Major" (to Joan) and Small Alison's classic AABA-format pop song format "Ring of Keys" all communicate different things sonically. When all the Alisons converge in "Flying Away," Kron and Tesori underline that all three are really one and the same even as they are also singular. This musicalized moment embodies what McMillin describes as "a shared musical formality even when characters are expressing their deep musical uniqueness. The characters are voicing themselves, yet they are joined by a formal element that lies beyond them. It exceeds their awareness."[29] McMillin locates this "beyond" in the orchestra, where it surely lies in part, but the "beyond" the characters that he writes about ineffably exists in the affect of both the actors and the spectators as well. They and we feel the formal elements at play without necessarily having to or even being able to articulate them. *Fun Home*, more than most musicals, taps into this ineffable "beyond."

On that note, a musical is more than just its text on the page and it is only in performance that a musical's multiple texts come fully alive. Part of what made *Fun Home*'s original production notable was the historic fact that Beth Malone, an out lesbian, played adult Alison—the first time an out lesbian played a lesbian lead in a Broadway musical. Bruce was played by Michael Cerveris, who is straight, which drew little criticism at the time perhaps because Bruce's sexuality is not so easily defined. Since the show's subject is very much about Alison's discovery of her sexuality and her coming out, commentators paying attention to casting and identity tended to focus on that role. There are so few lesbian roles in musical theatre and even fewer butch lesbian roles that the burden of representation fell more heavily on casting adult Alison than it did on Bruce; after all, musical theatre has many more gay male roles. At the time of *Fun Home*'s premiere, you could still count the number of lesbian leading roles in musicals on one hand.

Considering the scarcity of lesbian characters and the desire for so-called "authentic" casting, it was no shock when there was a small outcry when *Fun Home*'s US national tour cast former Miss America Kate Shindle as adult Alison. Shindle is straight and a vocal LGBTQ+ ally. She explained her feelings about doing the show, saying, "Not only those who consider themselves to be a part of the LGBTQ community, but also allies like me for example, need to link arms and say decisively that we are not going to go back to the world that killed Bruce Bechdel."[30] Shindle's bona fides as an ally were deep: when she was Miss America 1998, she spent her title year raising awareness and funds for HIV/AIDS across the US. As she told the *New York Times*, "because of what Miss America is, and was, to the country, people invited me places that no AIDS activist could get into" in the late 1990s.[31] If Shindle's casting raised eyebrows, it was her costume that made waves.

Shindle's look as Alison was different than Malone's, which caused a blogger known as "Spinster Woman" to publish a blog post claiming, "Of course I can only speculate, but I must wonder if former Miss America would . . . persuade [producers] to change her costuming to be more typically feminine. A butch lesbian just isn't relatable to most theatergoers, but a short-haired feminine lesbian might make the cut for tugging on those liberal heartstrings."[32] Shindle, sensitive to the politics of the situation, told an interviewer, "It just baffles me that anybody would think that [I] would sign on to [play] Alison Bechdel and say, 'you know what, I think we should femme her up a bit.'" She went on to note, "I really wanted to wear [the original costume] because it's so iconic. And nobody came out and said 'wow, that looks awful on you,' but judging by the speed at which other [costumes] started showing up in my dressing room, I kind of put two and two together."[33] Kron defended Shindle's casting and her costume on *Fun Home*'s website, where she wrote, "I feel good about the change in her costume. You may disagree. But was this decision, or any other, ever made to 'de-butchify' the show? No way. Not on this femme's watch."[34] The difference between Malone's costume (a maroon T-shirt with blue piping around the sleeves and neck) and Shindle's (a navy cardigan over a tank top and button-down shirt) became yet another of the musical's performance texts—just as the written components communicate meaning, so too do the elements of production like costume design.

Thinking about *Fun Home* raises several questions that deny easy answers: How does this show queer temporality? How do content and form work together to make *Fun Home* queer? If queer representation in musicals capitulates to or assimilates mainstream norms, is it still queer? If a musical has queer content but not a queer creator, is it still queer? Who gets to decide what counts as queer? Who gets to play Alison? Who should? And what should Alison wear? How do all of these choices taken together make or unmake queer approaches to a musical's various texts?

Notes

1 I have written elsewhere about the Broadway production's ambivalent embrace of its queer content in its advertising and Tony Awards performance. See Ryan Donovan, "If You Were Gay"; and ibid., *Broadway Bodies*.

2 Jaclyn I. Pryor, *Time Slips: Queer Temporalities, Contemporary Performance, and the Hole of History* (Evanston, IL: Northwestern University Press, 2017), 148.

3 Lisa Kron, interview with Laurie Winer, "How to Write a Musical."

4 Ibid.

5 Ibid.

6 Stacy Wolf, *Changed for Good: A Feminist History of the Broadway Musical* (New York: Oxford University Press, 2011), 203.

7 Jeanine Tesori and Lisa Kron, *Fun Home* (New York: Samuel French, 2014), 9.

8 Ibid., 17.

9 Ibid., 27.

10 Ibid., 45.

11 Ibid., 47.

12 Ibid., 56.

13 Ibid., 58.

14 Ibid., 60.

15 Ibid., 76.

16 Ibid., 77.

17 Stephen Sondheim, *Finishing the Hat: Collected Lyrics, (1954–1981)* (New York: Knopf, 2010), overleaf.

18 Tesori and Kron, *Fun Home*, 7.

19 Ibid., 8.

20 Ibid.

21 Lisa Kron, interview with Laurie Winer, "How to Write a Musical," *LA Review of Books*, June 7, 2015, https://lareviewofbooks.org/article/how-to-write-a-musical/.

22 Scott McMillin, The *Musical as Drama* (Princeton, NJ: Princeton University Press, 2014), 33.

23 Ibid., 208.

24 Sarah Whitfield, "Disrupting Heteronormative Temporality through Queer Dramaturgies: *Fun Home*, *Hadestown*, and *A Strange Loop*," *Arts* 9: 69. doi: 10.3390/arts9020069.

25 Ibid.

26 Tesori and Kron, *Fun Home*, 73.

27 Ibid., 74.

28 Ibid., 76.

29 McMillin, *Musical as Drama*, 71.

30 Kate Shindle, interview with Becs Richards, *Seattle Weekly*, July 12, 2017, https://www.seattleweekly.com/arts/kate-shindle-on-the-queer-activism-that-led-her-to-fun-home/.

31 Michael Paulson, "Union Boss (and Former Muss America) Hits the Road in 'Fun Home,'" *New York Times*, October 4, 2016, https://www.nytimes.com/2016/10/05/theater/union-boss-and-former-miss-america-hits-the-road-in-fun-home.html.

32 Quoted in Curtis M. Wong, "'Fun Home' Composer Hits Back at Claims Lesbian Character Was 'De-Butched,'" *Huffpost*, July 2, 2017, https://www.huffpost.com/entry/fun-home-tour -claims_n_5956abe8e4b0da2c73237c2b.

33 Kate Shindle, interview with Ryan Williams-Jent, *Watermark*, November 27, 2017, https://watermarkonline.com/2017/11 /27/kate-shindle-playing-author-alison-bechdel-national-tour -fun-home/.

34 Quoted in Wong, "'Fun Home' Composer."

3
Production
Cabaret

Cabaret (1966) is a musical whose initially obscured queerness has been brought to the surface most profoundly—though not only—in revival. This case study first addresses the original Broadway production before detailing changes to the show brought about by directors like Bob Fosse in his 1972 film adaptation and Sam Mendes in his 1993 revival at London's Donmar Warehouse and subsequent Broadway revivals. Composer John Kander, lyricist Fred Ebb, and librettist Joe Masteroff adapted *Cabaret* from two sources: Christopher Isherwood's fictionalized stories of his life in Weimar Berlin in the 1920s and 1930s and John Van Druten's 1951 play *I Am A Camera*, an earlier theatrical adaptation of Isherwood's stories. Isherwood himself never saw the stage musical though he did see Fosse's film, a heavily revised re-envisioning of the stage musical. He told an interviewer in 1974, "It was the book of the musical that I chiefly objected to," noting that the film was closer in spirit to the Berlin of his writing than the stage musical.[1] Fosse's film openly addressed sexuality in a way not entirely possible on stage just six years earlier, which was one likely reason why the film won

Isherwood's approval and the stage musical did not. A major difference between the 1966 stage production and 1972 film version of *Cabaret* was the fact that its male lead, Cliff, was renamed Brian, turned from an American ex-pat into a Brit, and was openly bisexual. Brian's coming out to his girlfriend Sally involved his admission that they'd both been sleeping with their mutual friend Max. Sally proclaims, "Screw Maximilian" and Brian responds, "I do."[2] This openness influenced later productions of the stage musical profoundly. *Cabaret* has proven a particularly flexible musical in this aspect, as well as with how it has taken liberty with regards to historical accuracy. Life may be a cabaret, old chum, but *Cabaret* is not life.

Despite the fact that characters burst into song, musicals still suggest realism rather than embody historical accuracy—or accurately embody history—and this is as true of *Cabaret* as it is of many musicals. The fact of the matter is that even Isherwood himself was not wholly faithful to history when writing the stories that would inspire the musical and would not attempt a greater degree of honest representation until a decade after the musical premiered in his 1976 memoir *Christopher and His Kind*. Isherwood's evasiveness in his books published in the 1930s (*Mr. Norris Changes Trains*, *Sally Bowles*, and *Goodbye to Berlin*) reveals the fact that an honest account *couldn't* have been published by a major publishing house then regarding what actually transpired in Weimar Berlin among his queer circle, just as a fully open representation of queer life in Berlin couldn't have been staged on Broadway in 1966, where mainstays like *Hello, Dolly!* (1964) and *Fiddler on the Roof* (1964) were settling into long runs. The offstage homosexual still held sway. *Cabaret* star Joel Grey explained, "But this was 1966, and a gay character on Broadway was not possible. So [Cliff] was to be a heterosexual American charmer."[3] If its subject matter was still edgy (if somewhat closeted in terms of sexuality), so was its form.

Critics and scholars widely cite *Cabaret* as one of the first so-called "concept musicals," which are organized around a concept rather than a traditional linear narrative. Yet, as Ebb later noted, "We didn't have the idea of a concept musical in mind when we were writing *Cabaret*."[4] *Cabaret* has a clear linear narrative—writer Cliff's arrival to and departure from Berlin via train open and close the narrative—in addition to its central metaphor. Despite its innovative framing and because it was still a commercial Broadway show, *Cabaret* used familiar musical theatre conventions, especially the use of two contrasting romantic couples (Rodgers and Hammerstein cemented this convention in musicals like *Oklahoma!* [1943] and *Carousel* [1945]). The leading couple, British chanteuse Sally Bowles and American writer Cliff Bradshaw, are both young expats whose ultimately failed romance parallels that of the secondary couple, landlady Fräulein Schneider and fruit seller Herr Schultz, two late-middle-aged Germans. That both romances end in separation comments on how the rise of Nazism split the fabric of German society on an interpersonal level. These romantic dissolutions also subvert then-dominant conventions of heteronormative coupling as the expected happy ending of a musical. Cliff arrives in Berlin seeking inspiration and shortly after his arrival he meets Sally at the Kit Kat Klub. They move in together at

Fräulein Schneider's boarding house for what will be a brief and tumultuous affair that ends with Sally's abortion and the dissolution of their relationship when Sally refuses to leave Berlin. Broadway audiences were not in *Oklahoma* territory any longer.

Schneider decides that she cannot risk her boarding house's business by marrying Schultz, because he is Jewish and thus a target of the Nazis. Cliff decides he must leave Berlin because he understands what's happening politically while Sally denies reality and insists on staying. While most musicals of the period ended with happy endings (often in marriages), *Cabaret* sent audiences out of the theatre on an ominous note with Cliff leaving Berlin by train—just as he entered the musical—and the Emcee materializing to sing a haunting reprise of the show's exuberant opening number, "Willkommen," interspersed with bits of dialogue from earlier scenes. This kind of fragmenting effect anticipates how *Fun Home* would employ this technique decades later. This scene culminates in Sally singing a fragment of the title song before the Emcee sings the show's last words, "Auf Wiedersehen! À bientôt! Good night!" an inversion of his first words, "Willkommen! Bienvenue! Welcome!"

Original *Cabaret* director Harold Prince, in collaboration with the show's writers, decided that the production would use the Weimar-era Berlin cabaret as a metaphor for the gradual rise of the Nazi regime. Thus, the Kit Kat Klub was conceived. The show's ingenious structure alternates between scenes and songs set both inside and outside of the Kit Kat Klub. The cabaret of *Cabaret* bore little resemblance to German Weimar-era *kabarett*. *Cabaret* biographer

Keith Garebian writes, "Broadway commercialism had something to do with the limits imposed on Prince's Kit Kat Klub. After all, if audiences were not considered ready for an explicitly homosexual male lead, they certainly were not ripe for exposure to the full flavor of Weimar cabaret, where the master of ceremonies often ran afoul of authority, with many . . . paying a brutal price at the hands of the Nazis."[5]

Cabaret opened a scant three years before the Stonewall riots would bring the existence of gay subculture to US national consciousness in June 1969. The original Broadway production closed just a couple of months after Stonewall, having been surpassed in topicality in many ways by the groundbreaking rock musical *Hair* (1967). *Hair* challenged sexual norms far more than *Cabaret*. *Hair*'s infamous nude scene and early, almost blink-and-you-miss-it representation of bisexuality in hippie subculture titillated Broadway audiences. *Cabaret*, too, was about an urban subculture that welcomed sexual minorities more openly than most in the 1920s. In the 1966 original Broadway production of *Cabaret*, a visible but silent queerness slipped through the cracks in a few powerful moments, in the stage directions and in the staging.

The final scene of the first act takes place in Herr Schultz's fruit shop, where a party is taking place celebrating his engagement to Fräulein Schneider. The party is disrupted when Ernst, whose chance meeting with Cliff on the train into Berlin at the top of the musical sets the narrative in motion, arrives wearing a Nazi armband. Ernst's arrival alone does not interrupt the dancing and festivities, but rather it is something Schultz notices that does: The stage directions indicate that Schultz "suddenly notes two boys dancing together. He looks around to see if anyone else has noticed)."[6] He immediately exclaims, "All right! Enough dancing! Enough! No more dancing." The act concludes with Ernst's warning to Fräulein Schneider that Schultz "is not a German," and though he does not say it is because Schultz is Jewish out loud, it is understood.

This moment of two boys dancing together was the original production's primary nod to the sexual subcultures thriving in late 1920s Berlin, and since it proved a turning point in that particular scene it shows that, despite Weimar Berlin's history as a haven for sexual outcasts, it was not universally the case that they were accepted before Hitler came to power. Apart from the sex worker Fräulein Kost, who "entertains" sailors (sometimes three at a time) in her flat in Schneider's building, the primary characters have romantic relationships that are decidedly heteronormative. Outside of these couplings sits the Emcee, one of the musical theatre's most iconic androgynous characters. And though the role has been played by cisgender men in all major Broadway and West End productions, the Emcee exists in a kind of liminal space throughout the musical (and even more so in later revivals than the original): the Kit Kat Klub, where nonnormative gender and sexuality are freely expressed.

The first burst of queerness in *Cabaret*'s original production is a momentary lapse in the opening number, "Willkommen," revealing a crack in the production's closet straightaway. The Emcee has just introduced the Kit Kat Klub's servers and is fussing with their dinner jackets when two identically dressed men enter from stage left (describing the original production's costumes, Garebian notes, "The costumes were deliberately cut to effect a bad or uncomfortably tight fit, and their androgynous look was quite congruent with the ambience of sexual experimentation. The female band were complemented by a pair of men in mated, dressy suits.") They are similar in size and appearance to Grey yet without his makeup. These men enter with exaggeratedly oversize swish gestures that read as camp. The first man blows a big kiss to the audience and skitters away, while the second greets the cabaret girls and the Emcee with over-the-top theatricality. Tantalizingly, they walk upstage for a brief moment and then the second stands behind the first and wraps his arms around him while Grey dances a short soft-shoe duet with another man in a seersucker jacket. At the duet's conclusion, this man rather brusquely walks upstage toward the couple and forces them to step aside in order for him to pass. The couple joins into the unison dancing that now takes over the number and they fade back into the ensemble. We never learn who these men are or what precisely their relationship to one another is, yet their physical intimacy indicates a close relationship—theirs is the only touch that contains any care in this opening number. This moment is brief yet noticeable if one is attuned to look for it. It offers a prime example of how gayness hid in plain sight in musicals in performance, extra-textually at least since these characters don't have names or even exist in the published libretto. It is telling to note that, in his memoir, Grey describes his nerves over performing at the Tony Awards, and his surprise that "the Broadway audience wholeheartedly embraced this little musical about Nazis, anti-Semitism, and homosexuals."[8] Queerness was there if you noticed it or knew what to look for but also easily missed if your eyes went elsewhere.

By the 1990s, it was not only possible but more desirable for musicals to be frank about sexuality, especially queer sexuality. It is therefore notable that the stage direction mentioned earlier is missing from the published version of the Sam Mendes/Rob Marshall revival that played the West End (1993) and Broadway (1998, 2014).[9] In 1966, this stage direction was as far as musicals were willing to push the limits of tolerance. Cliff was not bisexual yet (as he would become in the Mendes production) and the Emcee was a wickedly impish figure—*New York Times* critic Walter Kerr described original Emcee Joel Grey as "the silence of bad dreams, the gleeful puppet of pretended joy, sin on a string."[10] Grey's performance became legendary, and he went on to win the 1967 Tony Award for Best Performance by a Featured Actor in a Musical as well as the Best Supporting Actor Academy Award for his performance in Bob Fosse's 1972 film adaptation of the musical.

With his face slathered in white makeup and garish rouge painted on his cheeks, Grey made an arresting visual impact. His cheeky appearance coupled with his role as *Cabaret*'s amoral outsider/observer marked him as queer, especially in the sense of strangeness. His utterly stylized performance subverted gendered norms in both appearance and sound: he sang with a nasal and twangy "Broadway" style vibrato that nearly recalled a mixture of Ethel Merman's brassy vibrato and resonance with the vocal tessitura of a tenor. Throughout the musical, the Emcee treats the Kit Kat

Girls and their bodies as sex objects, yet he remains largely an asexual figure—these sexualized moments are always performance and directed to the audience as much as the onstage action. In original Broadway choreographer Ron Field's staging of "Willkommen" (as seen in its 1967 Tony Awards performance), when the Emcee proclaims that "each and every one" of the cabaret girls is "a virgin" and slaps one of the girls on her behind, he lets out a ferocious giggle and she smiles in a way that indicates the Emcee's gesture was harmless.[11] Later, "Two Ladies" comes across as a playful number commenting on the action occurring at Fräulein Schneider's boarding house rather than as an expression of the Emcee's sexuality. In the second act's opening number, the Emcee is revealed in drag among the kickline of cabaret girls—further queering the character.

The libretto's vagueness about the Emcee meant that it included not much more than a sketch of the character. In his memoir, Grey recalled, "there were no specific notations or descriptions in the script regarding my character. It didn't specify his connection to the narrative of the show or even if he had a name."[12] He understood the character "was clearly a metaphor for the corruption of the Weimar Republic" but noted that to "play a metaphor—not possible."[13] Grey discovered how he would play the role in a dream about a vulgar stand-up comic he had seen touring, and he also invented a backstory for the character since the libretto gave so little. He detailed the Emcee's sexuality, writing, "The Emcee wasn't just bisexual, he was any-and-every-sexual."[14] Grey filled in the outlines of the Emcee's past and also his "androgynous" look; the Emcee "was not trying to pass as a woman" despite passing as one in the kickline with the Kit Kat Girls in opening of the second act.[15]

Grey was the sole Broadway cast member to reprise his role in Fosse's heavily altered film version, which added new characters and subplots and entirely cut others from the stage musical. Grey's role survived and he even gained a new duet with the film's Sally Bowles, Liza Minnelli. When the original production was revived on Broadway in 1987 starring Grey again, one primary change was held over from Fosse's film: Cliff was now bisexual (at first).[16] Masteroff explains, "In the original production, Cliff was totally sexless. You couldn't have a gay leading man in those days. In the movie, he was bisexual. In the 1987 revival, as we traveled around the country, he was sort of bisexual. When we got to New York, we said, what the hell, let's make him a homosexual."[17] If this change was made possible by the profound shifts in US society following the 1969 Stonewall riots, it was also still a risk at a time when vast swaths of the US population viewed male bisexuality and homosexuality quite negatively due to homophobia, the stigma associated with HIV/AIDS, and the indifference or outright animosity of the US government under Ronald Reagan to gay people.

Cabaret's next major production came not from Broadway, but from London's Donmar Warehouse in 1993. Sam Mendes's production set a new standard for the darkness in the musical and its staging of queer sexuality. Garebian writes, "From theater setting to casting to choreography and stylization, this production was everything a revival was meant to be, except that it wasn't so much a revival as a daring, hypnotic, rethinking of the material."[18] The queering of this revival began when Mendes famously set its spectators inside the Kit Kat Klub itself, which took canny advantage of the Donmar's intimate and flexible layout to physically embody the original production's metaphor of the cabaret. No longer merely made complicit by the Kit Kat Klub mirror's reflection of the audience back to itself (as in Prince's Broadway version), this production positioned audiences themselves as the Kit Kat Klub's patrons.

This new spatial relationship with the audience was mirrored in the libretto, adapted for this production by Masteroff in collaboration with Mendes, who together "clarified the story by allowing all the characters—young, old, straight, gay, bisexual, and undecided—their sexuality."[19] Instead of the Emcee simply addressing the audience from inside the proscenium, he now talked to and engaged with them. This version of the libretto allowed for adlibbing by Alan Cumming as the Emcee, whose louche performance contrasted so much with Grey's take on the role that it was nearly a different character entirely. It was at the very least a radically reconfigured show, with changes to the libretto and the score (this production excised several songs from the original production in favor of others from the movie and one song initially cut from the show in 1966). Cumming's electric, star-making performance in the show tilted its balance to the point that the Emcee is much more present than in the original. He has many lines and frames the entire action, almost always watching over what happens onstage and sometimes popping into scenes and songs as an omniscient observer; instead of the cabaret being the organizing conceit, it's the Emcee himself. Cumming explained, "The emcee in this production is the overseer of the whole show and not just the club. The atmosphere of the evening is very much of his making. He's down and dirty. He's come up from the streets and he brings the streets with him. . . . And as the play progresses, with the rise of fascism, the emcee gets more and more debauched."[20] Cumming's performance helped transform *Cabaret* into something that spoke directly to audiences in the 1990s, who were accustomed to more edgy representations of queerness thanks to *Rent*.

Cumming's performance was leagues more "in your face" than Grey's was (or would have been permitted to be in 1966). There was more crotch grabbing in the opening number of the Mendes production than in probably every single 1960s Broadway musical combined. Cumming as the Emcee grabs the crotches of several musicians as well as his own throughout the show. Cumming noted in his diary of the early days of the show that "the choreography of my role consists of lots of touching the genitals of my fellow cast members (and a few twirls)."[21] In the *New Yorker*, Nancy Franklin described this production's attention to the groin, writing of Cumming's costume, "There is a bow tie, as befits a master of ceremonies, but it's attached to a parachute harness, which wraps around his body in a way that deliberately emphasizes his crotch. His nipples have been rouged and glittered, and he appears to have bruises on his torso. Cumming is a spectacle of mixed messages."[22] *Cabaret* was brazenly hedonistic and openly sexual.

It was now very openly queer from the get-go—gone were the swish but silent male couple of the 1966 production and gone were the tuxedos, too. In their places was a Kit

Kat Klub that was decidedly a dive rather than an elegant *boîte*—and one could grasp in earnest why Sally would need to sing a cheeky song like "Don't Tell Mama." Also new was the representation of queer sexualities beyond gay and bi men. Introducing the cabaret girls (and boys in this production) in "Willkommen," Cumming ad-libbed to a male audience member, "Texas. You like Texas? Well, too bad. 'cuz Texas likes girls."[23] The ensemble all played instruments and comprised the Kit Kat Klub's band, too, which further aimed to make audiences feel like they were inside the club rather than at the theatre. The queering of the lines between Kit Kat Klub and Broadway theatre made them blurry; the *New York Times* reported on "the naughty behavior of some customers at stageside tables who had apparently forgotten they were in a Broadway theater and not some strip joint from the pre-Disneyfied Times Square."[24] Cumming himself explained his approach to the Emcee's new relationship to the audience, telling a reporter about a moment when he chose audience members to join him onstage in a dance, "I always go for the butchest men because (the dance segment is) about humiliation in a way. The cabaret exists to unsettle the audience."[25] If Cumming aimed to disturb normative notions of gender or sexuality, this production's rupture of theatre's metaphorical fourth wall played a large part.

It wasn't just in the ad-libs that gay sexuality was to be found: the libretto's adaptation included new levels of frankness inspired by Isherwood's original writings. There's an entirely new character: Bobby, a waiter at the Kit Kat Klub, whose presence signals Cliff's queer past to audiences and to Sally when it's revealed that he and Bobby already know each other from The Nightingale Bar in London. Cliff and Bobby kiss onstage. Sally confronts Cliff, asking him, "Are you homosexual in any way? Bobby says you are."[26] This production took the film's advances even further now that it could.

Critics noted the impact of these changes to the musical. Clifford A. Ridley, writing in the *Philadelphia Inquirer*, noted, "This kind of unbridled license is what *Cabaret* always seemed to aim for but, in more circumspect times, only imperfectly achieved."[27] In a material way, the revisions that *Cabaret* underwent following 1966 were nearly always about un-closeting its queerness. The show's trajectory follows its source material and Isherwood's own attempts to tell his Berlin stories more authentically in print—first obliquely and then more openly when it was politically possible to do so. The Mendes/Marshall *Cabaret* was queered from beginning to end, which included the Holocaust in an attempt to make the ending more dramatic, even if it was historically inaccurate for the time of the show's setting. John Clum notes, "the final image is of the emcee in a concentration camp uniform ornamented with both the yellow star and the pink triangle."[28] Mendes's ending underlined the likely end that many denizens of the Kit Kat Klub would have met at the hands of Nazis.

Cabaret proves such a compelling object of studying queerness because of how the multiple contexts of its performance resonate with the musical's content and its setting. An interesting thing happened between its 1966 premiere and its 1990s revivals in that public acceptance of queer sexualities increased markedly and remaining closeted about one's sexuality became less common. It is important to note that the two actors most associated with the role of the Emcee, Grey and Cumming, both came out about their queerness, the former as gay in 2015 and the latter as bisexual in 1998. Grey came out when he was *de facto* retired, while Cumming's revelation was still something of a career risk when he did it, but unlike other actors who became pigeonholed and typecast after coming out, Cumming's career thrived. He later noted how his bisexuality was a plus for his career, telling the *Observer* in 2016, "I am the acceptable face of sexual ambiguity. I'm like a naughty schoolboy—I can get away with stuff, say stuff that's controversial. [. . .] I've done lots of heavyweight classy things. And I can dip my finger in trash quite easily."[29] What once would have been a liability was now a selling point. Just as *Cabaret*'s fictional character Cliff could now be out, so too can the actors playing him and other characters like the Emcee or Sally Bowles, for that matter. And the world largely yawned—more for Grey's announcement than Cumming's because bisexuality was (and is) still so misunderstood by the mainstream. As Fräulein Schneider might have said, "so who cares? So what?" *Cabaret*'s flexibility raises important questions about how musicals and queer representation evolve: Could *Cabaret* really be about homosexuals without any gay characters in it in 1966? How can and did performance emphasize queer elements that could not yet exist in the text? Should musicals be revised to reflect more contemporary understandings of the past when they are revived or should they attempt to show conditions as they were? What is the importance of casting out actors? Does theatrical truth matter more than historical accuracy in musicals?

Notes

1   CUNY TV, "Day at Night: Christopher Isherwood."

2   Quoted in Keith Garebian, *The Making of Cabaret*, 2nd ed. (New York: Oxford University Press, 2011), 140.

3   Joel Grey, *Master of Ceremonies: A Memoir* (New York: Flatiron Books, 2016), 152.

4   John Kander and Fred Ebb, *Colored Lights: Forty Years of Words and Music, Show Biz, Collaboration, and All That Jazz* (New York: Faber & Faber, 2003), 60.

5   Garebian, *The Making of Cabaret*, 54.

6   Joe Masteroff, John Kander, and Fred Ebb, *Cabaret* (New York: Random House, 1967), 78.

7   Garebian, *The Making of Cabaret*, 59.

8   Grey, *Master of Ceremonies*, 165.

9   Joe Masteroff, John Kander, and Fred Ebb, *Cabaret: The Illustrated Book and Lyrics* (New York: Newmarket Press, 1999).

10 Walter Kerr, review of *Cabaret* (Broadhurst Theatre), *New York Times*, November 21, 1966, 62.

11 Broadway Barfly, "Willkommen from CABARET ♪ (Joel Grey and cast, 1967 Tonys)," YouTube video (4:47), September 15, 2021, https://www.youtube.com/watch?v=OAZMLjT81cs.

12 Grey, *Master of Ceremonies*, 3–4.

13 Ibid., 4.

14 Ibid., 155.

15 Ibid.

16 Garebian, *The Making of Cabaret*, 159.

17 Masteroff et al., *Cabaret: The Illustrated Book and Lyrics*, 21.

18   Garebian, *The Making of Cabaret*, 164.

19   Linda Sunshine, Introduction to Joe Masteroff et al., *Cabaret: The Illustrated Book and Lyrics*, 13.

20   Quoted in Masteroff et al., *Cabaret: The Illustrated Book and Lyrics*, 109.

21   Ibid., 103.

22   Ibid., 72.

23   All references to the performance refer to the filmed version of the Sam Mendes Donmar Production: EnvyCentral, "Cabaret 1993—Mendes Production [feat Alan Cumming] (Full show)," YouTube video (1:46:33), January 28, 2019, https://www.youtube.com/watch?v=IOs82ubFyFQ.

24   Wilborn Hampton, "Very Busy Chorus Keeps 'Cabaret' On the Move; Singing, Dancing, Changing Scenery and Playing in the Band," *New York Times*, May 6, 1998, https://www.nytimes .com/1998/05/06/theater/very-busy-chorus-keeps-cabaret -move-singing-dancing-changing-scenery-playing.html.

25   Quoted in Masteroff et al., *Cabaret: The Illustrated Book and Lyrics*, 80.

26   Ibid.

27   Quoted in Ibid.

28   John Clum, *Something for the Boys: Musical Theater and Gay Culture* (New York: Palgrave, 1999), 279. Nazis made wear Jews the yellow star of David while the pink triangle denoted gay men.

29   Alan Cumming, interview with Adam Higginbotham, *The Observer*, February 16, 2003, https://www.theguardian.com/ books/2003/feb/16/fiction.film

4
Reception
La Cage aux Folles

Striking differences in the critical reception of *La Cage aux Folles* (1983) might surprise you. A profound gap existed between those who thought the musical's gay representation didn't go far enough and those who were grateful it existed at all. *La Cage* opened on Broadway on August 21, 1983, against an ever-increasing backdrop of plague and death as HIV/AIDS brutally ravaged the Broadway community, and gave Broadway audiences a farcical love story featuring gay men and drag queens almost as a balm against the terror of the real world. This case study addresses the reception of *La Cage* and how context and issues of representation informed the divergent responses to the musical, which exemplify the burdens of representation marginalized groups face as well as the binds in which representation places them.[1]

La Cage aux Folles is based on a 1973 French farce by Jean Poiret, and it tells the story of Georges and Albin, respectively the owner and the star of its titular drag nightclub. Mayhem ensues when Georges' son (from a youthful one-night stand) returns, announces he's marrying the daughter of a populist right-wing politician, and uninvites Albin from the "meet the parents" dinner since his estranged birth mother will attend in order to assist in the pretense that he is from a typical nuclear family. When his birth mother doesn't show, Albin dons drag and takes her place, making the show a mistaken identity farce, ultimately challenging (and paradoxically upholding) conservative family values.

When *La Cage*'s creative team (composer/lyricist Jerry Herman, book-writer Harvey Fierstein, and director Arthur Laurents) began working on the show, however, they had no way of knowing how serious AIDS would become as the show got on its feet. Nevertheless, they were blamed both by many heterosexual critics and by some gay activists for not responding more directly to the moment in which the musical opened. *La Cage* producer Barry Brown remembered that during the time they were putting *La Cage* together that AIDS "was a non-issue" in the show's creation.[2] Yet was it the artists' responsibility to predict—and rewrite their musical in response to—the tragedy unfolding offstage? Was there value in telling a joyful story with a happy ending at this time?

Fierstein was a vocal defender of the work that he saw *La Cage* doing ever since it first faced those critiques. In 2008, he squarely addressed the issue, saying:

The characters in *La Cage* are living their lives out loud and having a wonderful time. They are respected in their community. That is still not the case for many people today, and there are still politicians and religious leaders who make a living out of preaching hellfire on this, and as long as that is the case, *La Cage* has a role to play in the world. This show is very special to me. We lost half the cast of the first production to AIDS.[3]

He also noted how AIDS stigma functioned within the original company of *La Cage*, recounting that star Gene Barry "wouldn't get on an elevator with the chorus boys in *La Cage*."[4]

If the star of *La Cage* had such an attitude toward his fellow cast members, it is surprising that the majority of the mostly heterosexual mainstream media offered the show itself a much more accepting reception than Barry did to his cast-mates.

It may be difficult for readers to fully appreciate what the presence of *La Cage* on Broadway meant in 1983. While not the first Broadway musical to feature a gay male couple, it was the first to make them protagonists and, crucially, it was the first Broadway hit musical centrally *about* gay men. It was a risk for everyone involved, and its success was not assured. The creators knew they had to win over all audiences, straight and gay. Fierstein noted, "the gay politics were causing real battles here. People would be taking sides before they took their seats."[5] *La Cage*'s creative team confronted this anticipated division as they crafted the show. Laurents explains in his memoir that his approach "was rooted in my conviction that a large majority of the audience anywhere in the country (except San Francisco) was not gay-friendly [. . .] Despite all the drag, it was a family show."[6] The gay men writing the show perceived that homophobia would determine the musical's chances for success, but were less forthcoming about how homophobia also determined their own approaches to the show's gay content.

The burden of representation on the creators of *La Cage aux Folles* was heavy as it confronted several stigmas. The show's complexity existed because of—not despite—the specific context of 1983, which theatre historian Norman Hart noted as "a time when America was entering a period of neo-conservatism that was determined to reverse what it considered to be a decline in traditional family values."[7] *La Cage* cannily applied those family values to a middle-aged gay couple (in France—far enough away from the United States), even though these same values had been the antithesis of the gay liberation movement's rhetoric about the importance of gay visibility and free sexuality.

La Cage has consistently received contradictory responses, with mainstream critics faulting it—especially Fierstein's libretto—for not being authentic enough in its depiction of gays (as if there's only one way to be gay), while the gay press found more to applaud. *New York Times* critic Rich memorably called Georges and Albin "homogenized homosexuals."[8] Rich, who went on to become an advocate for gay equality during his years as an op-ed columnist for the *Times* after his long run as chief theatre critic, found *La Cage* so disappointing that he wrote another article six days later in which he explained his qualms at length. Rich's major criticism is that the creators were afraid of offending straight spectators with a more honest depiction of homosexuality. He notes that the "bigoted heterosexual villains of the piece [. . .] are so overdrawn that they seem calculated to make even the audience's homophobes go home congratulating themselves on how tolerant they are by comparison."[9]

Like Rich, other mainstream critics picked up on what they interpreted as the self-congratulatory tendencies of "liberal" straight audience members. Notoriously venomous critic John Simon argued that "[f]or the affluent, middle-class, middle-aged theatergoer there is a chance to feel wonderfully tolerant toward homosexuals, and tolerance is, of course, a good thing, though in this simplistic presentation it becomes really blindly patronizing smugness. . . . I fully expect straight couples to wear the ticket stubs of *Cage* as goody-goody-conduct medals."[10] He noted further that the musical was "beyond criticism" because audiences were so responsive to its charms. In the *New York Tribune*, Sy Syna went so far as to argue that, despite the message of "I Am What I Am," "homosexuals should repudiate this work because it reeks of homosexual self-loathing" and that "a sense of shame pervades much of this show." Syna, too, condemned both the politics of the show and its audiences: "But most of all, straights will adore this show as they do 'Torch Song Trilogy' because it allows them to sit back and laugh at the queers. Fags are figures of fun here. Never once are any of the issues concerning homosexuality seriously addressed."[11] Former *Times* critic Stanley Kauffmann, writing from his new perch at *Variety*, opined, "the audience cheers as if they all deserved Medals of Honor for social bravery."[12] Even Kauffmann faulted the musical for the universalizing logic of Fierstein's libretto, which he argued collapsed the vital differences of "homosexual life" into "mush." Historian Kaier Curtin contends, "Kauffmann's distortion of the musical does not really deserve serious consideration, except as another telling clue to the rationale behind the gay witch-hunt he helped foster."[13] In the *New York Post*, critic Clive Barnes felt that *La Cage* was "too apologetic for its homosexuality."[14]

Stigmatizing responses were often couched in reviews feigning disappointment at the clichéd depiction of the gay couple. UPI wire critic Glenne Currie posited that *La Cage* "was supposed to bring humanity to the gay scene, [but] is the most expensive piece of de-humanized camp ever to reach Broadway."[15] Currie's statement revealed that he viewed the "gay scene" as already lacking humanity, and also that he thought camp and humanity at odds with each other. He continues, "Much of the evening is devoted to depicting the sort of stereotyped homosexual queen the show was supposed to eliminate from the theater forever." Yet how was *La Cage* (or any musical) supposed to do that? This was a show about a drag queen, her male lover, and their son, after all. *New Yorker* critic Brendan Gill complained about *La Cage*'s "silly, constantly reiterated message to the effect that the family love practiced by homosexuals is somehow superior to the family love practiced by heterosexuals."[16] Gill missed entirely Fierstein's point that family love should be available to homosexuals as well as heterosexuals.

Robert Brustein's review in *The New Republic* carried the headline "Musicalized Propaganda," and it summed up many mainstream critics' contradictory, if largely positive, reactions to the show's form, even if they did not quite know what to make of the show's content or how to understand the terms of its politics. Typical of mainstream critics at this time, Brustein positioned gays in a binary, as either over-sexed or de-sexed through "flamboyance." Yet to his credit,

Brustein noted a compelling parallel between his alienation watching *La Cage* and that of gay people in the United States:

> I began this review by saying I felt alienated in the presence of this musical. I realize that this is nothing compared to the alienation experienced by most homosexuals in our society. Anything that reduces feelings of marginality and loneliness is by definition a positive accomplishment, and by that measure, I suppose, *La Cage aux Folles* is an effective piece of propaganda. Like most propaganda, however, it seriously misrepresents the cause it is advancing, and it is the homosexual community who will ultimately have to determine whether it is better served by "positive" and pretty evasions or by the unadorned and possibly "bleak" truth.[17]

That Brustein was unable or unwilling to see gay life as more than "possibly bleak" speaks as much to the social position of American gays in 1983 as it does to the limits of his own imagination.

A notable dissenter in the mainstream press was gossip columnist Liz Smith. Smith used her platform to champion the show—albeit from the closet, it must be noted, as she publicly came out as bisexual only in 2000. Her response thus admits her own stance toward gay politics as she cajoles, "Nertz to the carpers who wanted 'La Cage' to be more radical and innovative—what did they expect? A gay activist parade or a large sociological protest? 'La Cage' is a fabulous entertainment . . . and it would be wrenching things out of context to lob revolutionary grenades into the audience."[18] Despite the critical misunderstanding and misrecognition of *La Cage*'s politics, the reviews all admit the fact that the musical *was*, in fact, political—something the creators took great pains to avoid admitting in 1983.[19]

In the alternative and gay press (admittedly a much smaller sample of opinion than the mainstream press) responses to the original production of the musical were largely supportive, with a few notable exceptions emblematic of the criticism from the gay public that upset the creative team. The alternative and gay-friendly newspaper *SoHo News* and gay nightlife magazine *After Dark* had both closed (in 1982 and early 1983 respectively), leaving the *New York Native* and the *Village Voice* as the major alternative downtown New York press that regularly covered gay politics and the arts. The responses from the gay press show how a range of members of the communities represented onstage in *La Cage* responded to its representation. Gay men themselves would have been familiar with the performance of their sexuality for straight people and would have brought this awareness into the theatre with their critical eye. It was not only gays who understood the musical's politics, though; *Village Voice* critic Julius Novick, who was not gay, saw exactly what Fierstein was after. Rather than argue that *La Cage* missed the mark in its treatment of gays, he perceptively identified the balancing act that the musical performed in order to achieve Broadway success, noting that the show's very embrace of "ordinary middle-class values [. . .] enables it to achieve its mission of making the idea of homosexuality acceptable to the ordinary middle-class audience."[20]

The *Native* published several perspectives on *La Cage* that run the gamut from enthusiastic to skeptical. Most effusive of all was Terry Miller's review of the show, titled "Mascara Power." He wrote,

> For weeks you wondered: is *La Cage aux Folles* as good as you have heard? No. It's better. A lot of talented people worked very hard to create a fun '50s musical with a contemporary gay sensibility. The finished product is cause for celebration.[21]

Unlike critics in the mainstream press, Miller vividly appreciated new content (contemporary gay sensibility) placed in an old container (the 1950s musical) and wondered "why it wasn't tried thirty years ago." Miller also noted that the musical's way of dealing with sexuality made "points validating homosexuality [. . .] in the best possible way: without straining to do so."

The *Native* gave *La Cage* another review in its next issue. In his assessment, Michael Grumley noted an important aspect of the show: "In the twoness of *La Cage* is its magic: to see two men walking off into the sunset together, beneath the gilded arches of the Palace Theatre, is extremely satisfying."[22] Grumley acknowledged that the show contained numerous stereotypes but argued that it worked "not in spite of the clichés that abound, but rather because of them." These critics are notable for their generosity toward what the mainstream press viewed as the central weakness of the show: the stereotypical depiction of gays in Fierstein's libretto. In national gay news magazine *The Advocate*, critic Tish Dace wrote, "If *La Cage*'s glitter and whimsy are capable of sending audiences off into fantasy realms, the show also possesses a real power to turn trepidations about gay people into tolerance."[23] The gay press largely accepted the stereotypes as part and parcel of musicals; perhaps their expectations were lower since gay representation was itself still comparatively rare in 1983 and *La Cage* was decidedly affirmative—and all the gay characters are alive at the end of the show.

Not all of the critical responses from the alternative and gay press were as favorable or accepting of the musical, however. The *Native* published Richard Hall's dissent from the orthodox gay view of the show in his scathing indictment of both the musical and its audience, though for very different reasons than mainstream critics. He wrote, "The fact is, *La Cage* isn't a gay play at all, as it has presently evolved (with *Torch Song* a prime exemplar), and trying to fit it into some schema of gay theater or politics or contemporary gay behavior is utterly useless." Hall goes on to note that he began to hear "strange sounds" from the women around him in the audience: gasps, sighs, and sniffles. He initially assumed:

[T]he deep and powerful message of gay liberation, the universal dream of justice, has finally reached the mainstream middle-class heteros among whom I have been condemned to live my life. During intermission, the notion occurred to me that the audience's warm reaction was really their way of telling us they understood and sympathized with the AIDS crisis. Pass the hankie, please. . . . And then a small, skeptical voice whispered that they were moved not because we were dying of a sex-related disease but because they felt sorry for themselves. It was only a small step from there to the realization that *La Cage* appeals so broadly and deeply not because of its rather rudimentary message of gay liberation but because it is a profoundly redemptionist feminist allegory. It is a play in which woman-as-faggot comes to stand for the second-rate status of women, for all the injustices they have suffered at male hands. And who can represent women better than a drag queen—the metaphor *in extremis*—derided, mocked, persecuted, powerless?[24]

Hall concludes that this metaphor itself—not the musical's "message" or cunning casting of heterosexuals in its leading roles—was the real reason for its success. And while the message of *La Cage* can be read as a rudimentary gay liberation tale, it is more accurately read as an antecedent to the rise of gay equality politics.[25] The show has little, if anything, to say about feminism at all.

When *La Cage* premiered, most gays were still professionally closeted even if they were privately out. *Village Voice* columnist Arthur Bell was "the only openly gay person who wrote a weekly column in a widely circulated Gotham newspaper [so] he held sway over other homosexuals when it came to what they saw or didn't see on Broadway."[26] Bell wrote of some disappointed spectators' response to *La Cage*, "Expectations were too great. There was no way *La Cage Aux Folles* could have lived up to word of mouth." He, too, found the show's politics dated: "The politics of *Cage* are gay and proud, the message is very '60s-movement, but the male lovers never kiss. It's a lesson in tolerance, not brazenness, and should please all audiences—and that's a shame." Bell snuck into the opening night party and asked the musical's then-closeted composer-lyricist Jerry Herman whether he was "planning a pronouncement" in light of "I Am What I Am." Herman reportedly replied that the musical was not autobiographical.[27] While the show was neither autobiographical nor radical in its politics, it filled a gap in representation and paved the way for later musicals that *were* semi-autobiographical, radical, and openly queer like *A Strange Loop*.

Before the show became canonized, it sometimes occasioned protests and censorship. *La Cage* producer Barry Brown notes that the show's tour was the object of a protest in Buffalo in the 1980s.[28] This was surprisingly one of few protests that the musical received in its original production. Yet even the assimilationist family-friendly politics of the musical were not enough to stop the show from occasionally being censored. A 1989 Chicago area production was slapped with an "R-rating" because local district officials "believe that the play . . . may offend some with its story line and themes of homosexuality and transvestism."[29] Gay stigma had changed since 1983, yet it was still so keenly felt in 2007 that Fierstein wrote an op-ed for the *New York Times* detailing the position in which stigma left him. He writes, "Since I'm a second-class citizen—a gay man—my seats for the ballgame of American discourse are way back in the bleachers. . . . Hate speak against homosexuals is as commonplace as spam."[30]

As Fierstein noted of *La Cage* in 2008, "Society has changed around the show, but not sufficiently to render it any less meaningful than it was."[31] Public attitudes later changed, but during the height of AIDS hysteria in the 1980s many Americans felt that "homosexual relations between consenting adults" should be illegal.[32] The less tolerant public atmosphere makes its critical reception in the mainstream press that much more paradoxical in wishing for more accurate, more "authentic" gay representation. Or perhaps they just wanted gays to be more heteronormative and to have a little less fun.

London's West End was a particularly inhospitable environment for *La Cage* due to AIDS-panic and homophobia when it opened there in 1986. It was one of few places where the musical flopped (Australia was another) and *Variety* went so far as to suggest that there was "some speculation that the AIDS scare may have been a factor" in slow ticket sales.[33] Producer Brown agrees that the timing was unfortunate: "I do suspect that [AIDS] had something to do with a shortened run when we got to London, because AIDS had just gotten there, and it was on everybody's minds and everybody's lips, and I think a story about two men was not as well received as it might have been at another time."[34] The failure may have also had to do with the fact that the London Palladium was far too vast for the production with more than 600 seats than the show's Broadway home. The possibility also exists that British audiences simply found the show old hat given the long tradition of camp and drag in musical hall and panto shows.

The show failed to garner any nominations for the Olivier Awards, which prompted one reader, A. J. Tunstall, to write a letter to *The Stage* offering an unsolicited opinion as to why:

SIR, -Regarding the exclusion of La Cage Aux Folles from the Laurence Olivier Award nominations (Stage, Nov 13), may I be permitted to spell out the reason for this?

La Cage takes as its theme a blithesome look at a homosexual relationship, and for this won six awards in the USA. Since then however the public awareness of the growing peril of AIDS has brought to an abrupt end any idea of homosexuality being a suitable subject for a musical—however highly it is treated.

The philosophy: "Life's not worth a damn till you can say hey world, I am what I am," has wrought upon this planet a self-inflicted pestilence in which the innocent will perish with the guilty.

It is fortunate that the vast majority of the British public remain normal, solid and orthodox and regard sexual deviation as abhorrent.

The Olivier panel has obviously reflected this view and deserves every praise for having the guts to reject La Cage from its nominations.

La Cage is based on a totally unsavory premise and the sooner it ends, the better.[35]

Other readers responded vociferously to Tunstall's letter, prompting the *Stage* to print a full page devoted to their missives in support of the musical. Dennis Quilley, who was playing Georges in the West End, responded in kind:

SIR, Your correspondent Mr Tunstall, who praises the Laurence Olivier Awards panel for excluding La Cage from their nominations because of its homosexual themes (November 20) has allowed his very natural fear of AIDS to lead him into paranoia and bigotry.

Firstly, it is now surely common knowledge that AIDS is not exclusively a homosexual disease. . . . We are all in this together.

Secondly, nowhere does La Cage condone promiscuity—on the contrary it strongly advocates fidelity and monogamy and the tolerant, loving acceptance of people of differing lifestyles from one's own—precisely the human qualities needed at this time or indeed at any time.

Lastly, though it would not be surprising to read a letter of this crude and vindictive nature in certain areas of the daily press, it is sad to see it given such prominence in a paper with some pretensions to being the "House Journal" of a profession which could scarcely exist without the contribution of the gifted homosexuals who have always been—and hopefully always will be—among its most brilliant members.[36]

La Cage acted as a barometer for critics and spectators alike on either side of the Atlantic in the 1980s.

La Cage itself was reviewed with more fondness when it was revived on Broadway in 2004, directed by Jerry Zaks. Even cranky John Simon noted that despite the flaws of the 2004 revival, "none of this means that the show, endearingly old-fashioned as it is, can be dismissed as jerry-built or, worse yet, geriatric."[37] David Rooney, in *Variety*, situated the 2004 production in terms of its relevance to contemporary politics (while otherwise panning the production), writing, "In post-election 2004 America, musicals don't come with more built-in topicality than Jerry Herman's 'La Cage aux Folles,' which deals with homophobia and a political platform constructed on moral and family values."[38] Brantley's *New York Times* review focused on the sex appeal of the Cagelles, whom he found to be the most enticing aspect of the show.

The 2008 Menier Chocolate Factory/2010 Broadway revival received a nearly opposite reception to the 2004 one, in that it was praised for, as Brantley put it, "transforming a less-than-great musical into greatly affecting entertainment."[39] In the program for the 2008 British revival, Michael Coveney posited that the 1986 British production failed because "perhaps we were all AIDS-ed out by then."[40] Even though AIDS does not exist in the world of *La Cage*, it exists in the world where *La Cage* plays and this dissonance has, perhaps, overdetermined its reception. And yet *La Cage* still cannot be divorced from HIV/AIDS, ever-present in its absence from the musical. Understanding its reception in revival is also bound to this history: *La Cage*, now warmly greeted like an old friend, returns again and again while so many old friends lost to HIV/AIDS cannot. Despite their mixed receptions, both revivals won the Tony Award for Best Musical Revival, indicating both fondness for the musical within the industry itself and its commercial viability. *La Cage* seemed more relevant—and more pointedly political—in revival as the social position of gays in the United States had then changed only by degree and not by kind since few legal protections or rights had been enacted for LGBTQ+ people between 1984 and the early 2000s.

La Cage's reception changed accordingly, and the gay press began to write about the show with a newfound sense of recognition. A 2004 article from gay newspaper *The New York Blade* declared, "The subject is still as timely and urgent as it ever was—perhaps even more so now. The show arrives with an impeccable gay pedigree."[41] Writing about the 2010 revival, *New Yorker* critic Hilton Als felt director "[Terry] Johnson strips the Broadway from 'La Cage aux Folles' and gives the text, and the actors, a new dimension. His production is not the heterosexual's fantasia of gay life; it's something real, felt, and deep."[42] The status of *La Cage* was thus recuperated in the gay press, as well as by prominent gay critics. *La Cage*'s changing reception prompts consideration of several questions: What also gets revived with older musicals? How does sociocultural context determine reception? Who is the intended audience of queer representation? Why is it important to note the response of those from communities represented onstage? What can we glean about the historical status of queer people from then-contemporary critical stances?

Notes

1 See Ryan Donovan, *Broadway Bodies*, for an in-depth examination of *La Cage*.

2 Barry Brown (producer, *La Cage aux Folles*), in discussion with author, February 2018.

3 *La Cage aux Folles* program, Playhouse Theatre, London, UK, 2008.

4 Michel Kantor, director, episode 8 "Putting It Together: 1980–Present," *Broadway: The American Musical*, PBS, 2004.

5 Harvey Fierstein, *I Was Better Last Night* (New York: Alfred A. Knopf, 2022), 148.

6 Arthur Laurents, *The Rest of the Story: A Life Completed* (New York: Applause, 2011), 91.

7 Norman Hart, "The Selling of *La Cage aux Folles*: How Audiences Were Helped to Read Broadway's First Gay

Musical," *Theatre History Studies* 23 (June 2003): 5. Hart's article includes a compressed history of *La Cage*'s reception and while there is some overlap between our sources, the thrust of this chapter is quite different.

8   Frank Rich, review of *La Cage aux Folles*, *New York Times*, August 22, 1983.

9   Frank Rich, "Stage View: 'La Cage' Has That Old-Time Appeal," *New York Times,* August 28, 1983.

10 John Simon, review of *La Cage aux Folles*, *New York*, September 5, 1983.

11 Sy Syna, review of *La Cage aux Folles*, *New York Tribune*, August 22, 1983.

12 Stanley Kauffmann, review of *La Cage aux Folles*, *Saturday Review*, November–December 1983 (49–50); Robert Hofler, "Straight Talk about Gay Plays," *Variety*, July 23, 2001.

13 Kaier Curtin, *"We Can Always Call Them Bulgarians": The Emergence of Lesbians and Gay Men on the American Stage* (Boston: Alyson Publications, 1987), 331.

14 Clive Barnes, review of *La Cage aux Folles*, *New York Post*, August 22, 1983.

15 Glenne Currie, review of *La Cage aux Folles*, U.P.I., August 21, 1983.

16 Brendan Gill, review of *La Cage aux Folles*, *The New Yorker*, September 5, 1983.

17 Robert Brustein, review of *La Cage aux Folles*, *The New Republic*, September 19, 1983.

18 Liz Smith, *Liz Smith*, *New York Daily News*, August 23, 1983.

19 See Donovan, *Broadway Bodies*, chapter 4.

20 Julius Novick, review of *La Cage aux Folles*, *Village Voice*.

21 Terry Miller, review of *La Cage aux Folles*, *New York Native*, September 12, 1983.

22 Michael Grumley, review of *La Cage aux Folles*, *New York Native*, September 26, 1983.

23 Tish Dace, review of *La Cage aux Folles*, *The Advocate*, August 18, 1983.

24 Richard Hall, "The Pyschometrics of 'La Cage,'" *New York Native*, October 10, 1983.

25 See Donovan, *Broadway Bodies*, Chapter 4.

26 Robert Hofler, *Party Animals: A Hollywood Tale of Sex, Drugs, and Rock'n'Roll, Starring the Fabulous Allan Carr* (Boston: DaCapo Press, 2010), 174.

27 Arthur Bell, "Bell Tells" column, *Village Voice*, August 30, 1983.

28 Brown, discussion.

29 "Our Towns: A Community Notebook," *Chicago Tribune*, August 27, 1989.

30 Harvey Fierstein, "Our Prejudices, Ourselves," *New York Times*, April 13, 2007.

31 "Who They Are: Michael Coveney in conversation with Jerry Herman and Harvey Fierstein," *La Cage aux Folles* program, Playhouse Theatre, London, UK, 2008.

32 "Gay and Lesbian Rights," *Gallup*, accessed April 5, 2018, http://news.gallup.com/poll/1651/gay-lesbian-rights.aspx.

33 "London Critics Pan West End 'La Cage,'" *Variety*, May 14, 1986.

34 Brown, discussion.

35 A. J. Tunstall, letter to the editor, *The Stage and Television Today*, November 20, 1986. Punctuation in original.

36 Dennis Quilley, letter to the editor, *The Stage and Television Today*, n.d. (n.b., this letter to the editor presumably appeared in the issue following the issue of November 20, 1986).

37 John Simon, review of *La Cage aux Folles*, *New York*, December 20, 2004.

38 David Rooney, review of *La Cage aux Folles*, *Variety*, December 9, 2004.

39 Ben Brantley, review of *La Cage aux Folles*, *New York Times*, April 18, 2010.

40 *La Cage aux Folles* program, Playhouse Theatre, London, 2008.

41 Steve Weinstein, "Just in Time: 'La Cage' Returns," *New York Blade*, December 10, 2004.

42 Hilton Als, review of *La Cage aux Folles*, *The New Yorker*, May 3, 2010.

Conclusion

This book has raised many questions about the complexity of the relationship between queerness and musical theatre's past, present, and future. I hope these questions prompt your own discoveries. This short study is a starting point, not the end of the story—it can indeed only highlight some parts of musical theatre's relationship to queerness and I have focused on musicals that played Broadway or the West End at the expense of Off-Broadway and beyond. Queerness evolves and expands, whether the world accommodates and includes queer people or not. We are here to stay.

Queer approaches in musical theatre continually push the form in new directions. Sometimes this means new bodies in old roles and sometimes new roles in old vehicles. An example of the latter is the "LGBTQIA+ focused rewrite" of *The Fantasticks* (1960), which "features two young gay men at the center of the story" in the place of the traditional cisgender, heterosexual couple.[1] For an example of the former, the 2022 national tour of Daniel Fish's experimental revival of *Oklahoma!* featured two trans actors, Sis and Hennessy Winkler, as Ado Annie and Will Parker, respectively.[2] That both productions were happening outside of New York speaks to the degree that musical theatre's queerness is now so open that this queered *Oklahoma!* can now play in Kansas City and bring things "up to date" there—a thought unimaginable even at the turn of the twenty-first century. When this happens on Broadway or in the West End with regularity, it will be clear a shift has occurred.

Though this book has focused on queer approaches to musical theatre in the Anglophone world, it would be remiss of me not to at the very least nod to the fact that this is only part of the picture. It is not just United States and United Kingdom-based writers who are taking queer approaches to musicals. the original Filipino musical *Care Divas—An Original Pinoy Musical* (2010) embodies the global appeal of queer musicals (and like *La Cage* and so many others, *Care Divas* features drag queens). *Care Divas* is about the clash of cultures, and as scholar Sir Anril Tiatco explains, the show "revolves around the struggle of five Filipino caregivers in Israel. However, this struggle is a mere background to the real struggle with their sexual identities as *bakla* (Filipino gay men) in this predominantly Jewish nation."[3] The two words in the show's title mirror the split lives of the five men: they work as caregivers during the day and drag queens at night. Tiatco argues that the show "implicitly featured the Filipino homosexual as a cosmopolitan." *Care Divas* stages queer identities that are explicitly transnational and that also contain the potential to mitigate the clash of cultures—through drag!

Another musical about the clash of cultures—in this case, gay drag queen culture and working-class, heterosexual Britain—the smash hit *Everybody's Talking About Jamie* (2017) first opened at the Crucible Theatre in Sheffield,

England before transferring to the West End nine months later. Based upon a true story, *Jamie* depicts what happens to a gay fifteen-year-old when he realizes he wants to be a drag queen and how his mum and community come together to support him. Jamie overcomes the school bully and triumphs, set to a catchy pop-inflected score by Dan Gillespie Sells and Tom MacRae. *Jamie*'s subject matter and its exuberance resonated with audiences beyond the UK and not in English: replica productions of the show were staged in translation in Korea and Japan in 2021 and Italy in 2022.

Queerness signifies differently in different places, yet *Jamie*'s success beyond its culture of origin speaks to how specifically queer stories can sing universal truths; the critic for the *Korea Herald* noted, "Unlike many other musicals, featuring damsels in distress and doomed love stories, 'Jamie' is all about self-realization."[4] This queer approach to musical theatre transcended its beginnings and sent a message of empowerment available to anyone willing to receive it. In a sign of the times, K-pop boy band stars MJ and Ren were two of the four actors who shared the title role in Korea—it was not career suicide for these stars to play a gay drag queen. A 2021 film adaptation of *Jamie* further evinces that affirmatively queer musicals—the drag queen triumphs as the bully's bravura is punctured, nobody dies—can be global commercial phenomena, too. And they can be fun, smart, searing, sad, incisive, and inclusive. In short, queerness in musicals no longer exists solely to entertain or provide comfortable representations geared only to mainstream audiences. Queer approaches to musicals now speak directly to queer audiences around the world. *Jamie* dared to show a happy ending for the queer characters and showered audiences with self-actualization in stilettos.

If *Jamie* was part of changing traditional gender roles in musical theatre, industry paradigms increasingly moved to include nonbinary, gender nonconforming, and trans performers in musicals like *A Strange Loop*, *& Juliet*, and *Some Like It Hot*. L. Morgan Lee made history as the first trans performer nominated for Best Performance by an Actress in a Featured Role in a Musical for her work in *A Strange Loop* in 2022. Lee told the *New York Times* that the show's success "means that there is hope. I'm careful with the word change, because in order for us to be in the type of world and space we want to be in, it's not as much about change as much as it is about growth."[5] Hope is what queer approaches in musical theatre represent—hope for more inclusive societies, an end to oppression, a better world, and the perennial hope that, in the words of *Jamie*, "there's a place where we belong."

Notes

1   Andrew Gans, "*The Fantasticks* Creator Tom Jones Rewrites Classic Musical as Gay Love Story, Premiering in June in Michigan," *Playbill*, May 17, 2022, https://www.playbill.com /article/the-fantasticks-creator-tom-jones-rewrites-classic -musical-as-gay-love-story-premiering-in-june-in-michigan.

2   Cameron Kelsall, "Trans Actors Take the Stage in 'Oklahoma!' National Tour," *Philadelphia Gay News*, March 8, 2022, https://epgn.com/2022/03/08/trans-actors-take-the-stage-in -oklahoma-national-tour/.

3   Sir Anril Tiatco, "PETA's 'The Care Divas' and the Ethics
    of Care," *The Theatre Times*, March 11, 2017, https://
    thetheatretimes.com/petas-care-divas-ethics-care/.

4   Im Eun-byel, review of *Everybody's Talking About Jamie*, *Korea
    Herald*, July 28, 2020, https://www.koreaherald.com/view.php
    ?ud=20200728000714.

5   L. Morgan Lee, interview with Matt Stevens, *New York Times*,
    May 9, 2022, https://www.nytimes.com/2022/05/09/theater/l
    -morgan-lee-a-strange-loop-tonys.html.

References

2016 Broadway Revival Cast. *Falsettos* (2016 Broadway Cast Recording). 2016. Sh-K-Boom Records, Inc. and Lincoln Center Theater, streaming.

Als, Hilton. Review of *La Cage aux Folles*. Longacre Theatre, New York. *New Yorker*, May 3, 2010.

Ashley, Christopher, dir. *Diana the Musical*. 2021. Los Gatos, CA: Netflix, streaming.

Barbaro, Michael. "This Drug Could End H.I.V. Why Hasn't It." Produced by *New York Times*. *The Daily*. June 5, 2019. Podcast, 29:42. https://www.nytimes.com/2019/06/05/podcasts/the -daily/hiv-aids-truvada-prep.html.

Broadway Barfly. "Willkommen from CABARET ♪ (Joel Grey and Cast, 1967 Tonys)." YouTube video (4:47), September 15, 2021. https://www.youtube.com/watch?v=OAZMLjT81cs.

Brown, Barry. Discussion with Author. Digital Recording, February 2018.

Chomsky, Daniel and Scott Barclay. "The Editor, the Publisher, and His Mother: The Representation of Lesbians and Gays in the *New York Times*." *Journal of Homosexuality* 60 (2013): 1389–408.

Clum, John. *Something for the Boys: Musical Theater and Gay Culture*. New York: Palgrave, 1999.

Colden Lamb. "LADY IN THE DARK Segment from MUSICAL COMEDY TONIGHT." YouTube video (12:12). January 7, 2022. https://www.youtube.com/watch?v=EuoBouVaPyQ&t=1s.

CUNY TV. "Day at Night: Christopher Isherwood." YouTube video (28:35). January 13, 2011. https://www.youtube.com/watch?v=kx09mDenhKU.

Curtin, Kaier. *"We Can Always Call Them Bulgarians": The Emergence of Lesbians and Gay Men on the American Stage*. Boston: Alyson Publications, 1987.

Donovan, Ryan. *Broadway Bodies: A Critical History of Conformity*. New York: Oxford University Press, 2023.

Donovan, Ryan. "If You Were Gay, That'd Be Okay: Marketing LGBTQ Musicals from *La Cage* to *The Prom*." In *Gender, Sex and Sexuality in Musical Theatre: He/She/They Could Have Dance All Night*, edited by Kelly Kessler. Bristol: Intellect, 2023.

Duggan, Lisa. "The New Homonormativity: The Sexual Politics of Neoliberalism." In *Materialising Democracy: Towards a Revitalized Cultural Politics*, edited by R. Castronovo and D. D. Nelson, 175–94. Durham, NC: Duke University Press, 2002.

EnvyCentral. "Cabaret 1993 – Mendes Production [Feat Alan Cumming] (Full Show)." YouTube video (1:46:33). January 28, 2019. https://www.youtube.com/watch?v=IOs82ubFyFQ.

Fierstein, Harvey. *I Was Better Last Night: A Memoir*. New York: Alfred A. Knopf, 2022.

Fierstein, Harvey and Jerry Herman. *La Cage aux Folles*. New York: Samuel French, 1984.

Forsgren, La Donna L. "*The Wiz* Redux, or Why Queer Black Feminist Spectatorship and Politically Engaged Popular Entertainment Continue to Matter." *Theatre Survey* 60, no. 3 (2019): 325–54.

Franke, Caroline. "Why *Rent* Feels so Outdated 20 Years After Its Debut." *Vox*, April 29, 2016. https://www.vox.com/2016/4/29 /11531350/rent-musical-20th-anniversary.

Gallup. "Gay and Lesbian Rights." http://news.gallup.com/poll /1651/gay-lesbian-rights.aspx (Accessed April 20, 2018).

Gans, Andrew. "*The Fantasticks* Creator Tom Jones Rewrites Classic Musical as Gay Love Story, Premiering in June in Michigan." *Playbill*, May 17, 2022. https://www.playbill.com /article/the-fantasticks-creator-tom-jones-rewrites-classic -musical-as-gay-love-story-premiering-in-june-in-michigan.

Garebian, Keith. *The Making of Cabaret*, 2nd ed. New York: Oxford University Press, 2011.

Gilchrist, Tracy E. "*Falsettos*' Story of Love & Family Amid the Onset of AIDS is Timeless." *Advocate*, April 2, 2019. https:// www.advocate.com/theater/2019/4/02/falsettos-story-love -family-amid-onset-aids-timeless.

Gordon, Robert Olaf Jubin, and Millie Taylor. *British Musical Theatre since 1950*. London: Bloomsbury Methuen Drama, 2016.

Grey, Joel. *Master of Ceremonies: A Memoir*. New York: Flatiron Books, 2016.

Gross, Larry. *Up from Invisibility: Lesbians, Gay Men, and the Media in America*. New York: Columbia University Press, 2001.

Halperin, David M. *How to Be Gay*. Cambridge, MA: Harvard University Press, 2014.

Hart, Moss, Ira Gershwin, and Kurt Weill. "Lady in the Dark." In *Great Musicals of the American Theatre*, volume 2, edited by Stanley Richards, 72–162. Radnor, PA: Chilton Book Company, 1976.

Hart, Norman. "The Selling of *La Cage aux Folles*: How Audiences Were Helped to Read Broadway's First Gay Musical." *Theatre History Studies* 23 (June 2003): 5–24.

Hofler, Robert. *Party Animals: A Hollywood Tale of Sex, Drugs, and Rock'n'Roll, Starring the Fabulous Allan Carr*. Boston: DaCapo Press, 2010.

Ickes, Bob. "Rent Decrease." *Poz*, October 1, 2008. https://www.poz.com/article/rent-broadway-hiv-15305-8144.

Im Eun-byel. Review of *Everybody's Talking About Jamie*. Korea Herald, July 28, 2020. https://www.koreaherald.com/view.php?ud=20200728000714.

Kander, John and Fred Ebb as told to Greg Lawrence. *Colored Lights: Forty Years of Words and Music, Show Biz, Collaboration, and All That Jazz*. New York: Faber and Faber, Inc., 2003.

Kantor, Michael. *Broadway: The American Musical*. Episode 8 "Putting It Together: 1980–Present." PBS, 2004. DVD.

Kass, Deborah. "Feel Good Paintings for Feel Bad Times." https://deborahkass.com/feel-good-paintings.html.

Keating, Joshua. "1987: The Year The *New York Times* Discovered Gay People." *Slate*, October 11, 2013. http://www.slate.com/blogs/outward/2013/10/11/the_new_york_times_discovered_gay_people_in_1987.html.

Keeley, Matt. "Theatergoer Walked Out of 'Rent' Because the 'Show Was About Gays.'" *Newsweek*, March 14, 2022. https://www.newsweek.com/theatergoer-walked-out-rent-because-show-was-about-gays-1687962.

Kirle, Bruce. *Unfinished Show Business: Broadway Musicals as Works-in-Process*. Carbondale, IL: Southern Illinois University Press, 2005.

Kron, Lisa. Interview with Laurie Winer. "How to Write a Musical." *LA Review of Books*, June 7, 2015. https://lareviewofbooks.org/article/how-to-write-a-musical/.

La Cage aux Folles Program. "Who They Are: Michael Coveney in Conversation with Jerry Herman and Harvey Fierstein." Playhouse Theatre, London, 2008.

Laurents, Arthur. *The Rest of the Story: A Life Completed*. New York: Applause, 2011.

Mantoan, Lindsey. "The Utopic Vision of OSF's *Oklahoma!*: Recuperative Casting Practices and Queering Early American History." *Studies in Musical Theatre* 15, no. 1 (2021): 41–56.

Masteroff, Joe, John Kander, and Fred Ebb. *Cabaret*. New York: Random House, 1967.

Masteroff, Joe, John Kander, and Fred Ebb. *Cabaret: The Illustrated Book and Lyrics*. New York: Newmarket Press, 1999.

McCann, Hannah and Whitney Monaghan. *Queer Theory Now: From Foundations to Futures*. London: Bloomsbury, 2019.

McMillin, Scott. *The Musical as Drama*. Princeton, NJ: Princeton University Press, 2014.

Miller, D. A. *Place for Us: Essay on the Broadway Musical*. Cambridge: Harvard University Press, 1998.

Original Broadway Cast. "Rent." *The Best of Rent*. 1999. SKG Music, LLC, streaming.

Original Broadway Cast. *The Book of Mormon* (Original Broadway Cast Recording). 2011. Ghost Light Records, streaming.

Original Cast. *A Strange Loop* (Original Cast Recording). 2019. Yellow Sound Label, streaming.

Pryor, Jaclyn I. *Time Slips: Queer Temporalities, Contemporary Performance, and the Hole of History*. Evanston, IL: Northwestern University Press, 2017.

Rogers, Bradley. "The Queer Pleasures of Musicals." In *The Oxford Handbook of Music and Queerness*, edited by Fred Evertt Maus and Sheila Whiteley, 63–80. New York: Oxford University Press, 2022.

Sandoval-Sánchez, Alberto. *José, Can You See?: Latinos On and Off Broadway*. Madison, WI: The University of Wisconsin Press, 1999.

Savran, David. *A Queer Sort of Materialism: Recontextualizing American Theater*. Ann Arbor, MI: University of Michigan Press, 2003.

Schildcrout, Jordan. "Drama and the New Sexualities." In *The Oxford Handbook of American Drama*, edited by Jeffrey H. Richards and Heather S. Nathans, 455–9. New York: Oxford University Press, 2014.

Schulman, Sarah. *The Gentrification of the Mind: Witness to a Lost Imagination*. Berkeley, CA: University of California Press, 2012.

Simpson, Janice C. "The Root: Is Broadway's 'Book of Mormon' Offensive?." *NPR*, April 15, 2011. https://www.npr.org/2011/04/15/135437800/the-root-is-broadways-book-of-mormon-offensive.

Smithsonian.com. "As an African American, LGBTQ+ Woman, Ethel Waters Shaped U.S. Entertainment." *Because of Her Story (The Smithsonian)*. June 12, 2020. https://womenshistory.si.edu/news/2020/06/african-american-lgbtq-woman-ethel-waters-shaped-us-entertainment.

Solomon, Alisa. "What Does It Mean to Remember AIDS?" *Nation*, November 30, 2017. https://www.thenation.com/article/archive/what-does-it-mean-to-remember-aids/.

Sondheim, Stephen. *Finishing the Hat: Collected Lyrics, (1954–1981)*. New York: Knopf, 2010.

Tesori, Jeanine and Lisa Kron. *Fun Home*. New York: Samuel French, 2014.

Tiatco, Sir Anril. "PETA's 'The Care Divas' and the Ethics of Care." *The Theatre Times*, March 11, 2017. https://thetheatretimes.com/petas-care-divas-ethics-care/.

Whitfield, Sarah. "Disrupting Heteronormative Temporality Through Queer Dramaturgies: *Fun Home*, *Hadestown*, and *A Strange Loop*." *Arts* 9: 69. doi: 10.3390/arts9020069.

Wolf, Stacy. *Changed for Good: A Feminist History of the Broadway Musical*. New York: Oxford University Press, 2011.

REFERENCES

Wollman, Elizabeth L. *Hard Times: The Adult Musical in 1970s New York City*. New York: Oxford University Press, 2013.

Wollman, Elizabeth L. "Musical Theater Studies: A Critical View of the Discipline's History in the United States and the United Kingdom." *Music Research Annual* 2 (2021): 1–29.

Wong, Curtis M. "'Fun Home' Composer Hits Back at Claims Lesbian Character Was 'De-Butched.'" *Huffpost*, July 2, 2017. https://www.huffpost.com/entry/fun-home-tour-claims_n_595 6abe8e4b0da2c73237c2b.

Index

INDEX